THE CHURCH OF ENGLAND IN CRISIS

THE
CHURCH OF ENGLAND
IN CRISIS

TREVOR BEESON
Vicar of St. Mary's Parish Church, Ware

DAVIS-POYNTER
LONDON

First published in 1973 by
Davis-Poynter Ltd
10 Earlham Street
London WC2H 9LP

ISBN 0 7067 0058 9 (cased)
ISBN 0 7067 0060 0 (paperback)

Printed in Great Britain by
Bristol Typesetting Co Ltd
Bristol and London

TO JO, JEAN AND CATHERINE
WHOSE PATIENCE WITH THE AUTHOR
DURING HIS WRITING OF THIS BOOK
OFFERED INCONTROVERTIBLE EVIDENCE
THAT EVEN IN A TIME OF CRISIS
THE CHURCH OF ENGLAND CONTINUES
TO PRODUCE ITS SAINTS AND HEROES

CONTENTS

		page
Chapter One	A CHURCH COMPREHENSIVE AND DIVIDED	9
Chapter Two	PEOPLE AND PROPERTY	24
Chapter Three	THE STATISTICS OF DECLINE	40
Chapter Four	PARISHES AND PRIESTS	54
Chapter Five	LITURGY AND CHAOS	70
Chapter Six	BEAUTY IN BANDS	93
Chapter Seven	TRIAL BY SYNOD	114
Chapter Eight	TREASURE ON EARTH	135
Chapter Nine	INFLUENCE AND INFLUENCERS	161
Chapter Ten	REALITY AND LOCALITY	177
Index		190

chapter 1

A Church Comprehensive and Divided

Shortly before six o'clock in the afternoon of 3 May, 1972, the Archbishop of York, Dr. Donald Coggan, announced to the General Synod of the Church of England the result of its voting on a scheme designed to unite the Established Church and the Methodist Church. Bishops, clergy and laity had, in accordance with the pre-scribed procedure, voted separately. Dr. Coggan delivered their verdict:

Bishops	34 for,	6 against (85 per cent in favour)
Clergy	152 for,	80 against (65.52 per cent in favour)
Laity	147 for,	87 against (62.82 per cent in favour)

Had the voting involved the elected representatives of the British people, meeting across the road in Parliament to decide on a matter of crucial importance for the future of the nation, say, entry into the European Economic Community, the result would have been a triumph for the government. Not so for the Church of England which had decided earlier that acceptance of the Anglican-Methodist unity proposals required two-thirds majorities in each of the three houses of the General Synod and an overall majority of 75 per cent. Thus sixteen years of patient – most would say tedious – negotiation ended in defeat for those in the Church of England who wished to see their church reunited with a smaller church from which it had been separated for more than 200 years.

Although 3 May was a delightful spring day in London, with warmth and signs of new life evident everywhere, it was a bleak and gruelling day for the 500 Synod members. But observers of this historic occasion were, within a space of eight hours, presented with a vivid picture of the

main areas of crisis in England's national church. By the
end of the day the more perceptive among the 333 frustrated voters were aware that they had been involved
in an event which had not only destroyed a cherished
hope but also exposed, most painfully, the nature of the
sickness now afflicting a great Christian institution. The
Archbishop of Canterbury, Dr. Michael Ramsey, was fore-
most among those who recognized the dangerous malady
underlying the symptoms and was unable to conceal his
anxiety at the press conference which followed the
verdict.

Words like 'crisis' and 'sickness' must, however, be
handled with great care when discussing the affairs of
the Church of England, or indeed the life of the Christian
church as a whole. In the same way that experienced
political commentators are careful never to forecast
election results, so those who comment on the ecclesiastical scene must – if they take history seriously – resist the
temptation to announce the impending demise of the
church. Fourteen centuries have passed since Pope Gregory the Great described the church as 'an old and worm-
eaten ship afloat on the deep, breaking up as in a ship-
wreck'[1] and even the most hostile critic of the contemporary church is obliged to admit that the worms have
been slow eaters and the process of break-up somewhat
protracted. Many other worthy institutions have been
born and buried since Gregory offered unmistakable
evidence of papal fallibility.

An informed discussion of the churches is bound to
take serious account of their resilience. Disorder, corruption and inertia are deplorable and painful symptoms
in a body committed to the promotion of that which is
most creative in human life, but they are not always
indications of terminal illness, as the history of the
church, from New Testament times onwards, clearly
shows. Those who lament the present condition of the
Church of England – this book will not attempt to dis-
guise the reasons for heartbreak – would do well to
reflect from time to time on the condition of the same

[1] *Epistles* i.4.

church for the greater part of the 18th century when the situation was in almost every way more alarming. Others who believe that the church in England and elsewhere is now in its death throes might profitably consider the likely contents of a first century volume titled *The Church of Corinth in Crisis*. If the fragmentary evidence of Paul's letters is a reliable guide, the book would be as incredible as it was deplorable in its revelations.

Theologians, preachers and ecclesiastical statesmen are apt to ascribe the resilience of the church to its divine origin and subsequent protection: 'The gates of hell shall not prevail against it'. This may be so, but in the nature of the case it cannot be proved, and when the doctrine is applied to particular situations it may easily breed dangerous complacency. The church enjoyed a golden age in North Africa from the 2nd to the 7th century, spreading to every part of the ancient Roman province and producing a lavish crop of saints, martyrs and theologians. By the early part of the 5th century it was strong enough to support 300 bishops and there was ample encouragement for those who believed in the inevitability of Christian expansion. But all was swept away by the Muslim invasions of the 7th century and it was not until 1881 that Christian missionaries ventured again into North Africa. Their progress since then has been minimal and the church has not yet been re-established in the lands of St. Augustine and St. Cyprian.

Those whose lack of inspiration, confidence or facts makes them reluctant to speak of divine protection of the church, may settle instead for the not unreasonable view that the church is dealing with a 'commodity' which has at its heart an element of permanence, i.e. man's quest for meaning and hope of immortality, and that over the course of the centuries the church has, like an animal born in the jungle, learned the art of survival. Certainly it would be most unwise to underestimate the staying power of the Church of England and, although this book will attempt to analyse the church's current crisis and to diagnose its present sickness, it is necessary to proceed on the assumption that the subject of the enquiry will still be available for further investigation during the

opening decades of the 21st century. The undertaker must
wait yet awhile, which will be a profound relief to most
Anglicans but an equally profound disappointment to
some others who believe that the revival of the Christian
religion in this country will be delayed until the ancient
ecclesiastical structures are buried.

These structures were plainly visible on the occasion
of the Anglican-Methodist unity decision. The day began
with members of the General Synod assembling in St.
Margaret's Church, Westminster for a celebration of the
Holy Communion. The Church of England is still ready
to accord priority to devotion of a decent and orderly
kind. It would have seemed improper for the General
Synod to have embarked upon so momentous a day's
work without invoking the guidance of God, notwithstanding the fact that all but a mere handful of those
who would vote had already made up their minds what
they were going to do. Those responsible for ordering the
service were careful to avoid any hint that they might
be attempting to brain-wash the worshippers into acceptance of the unity scheme. Whatever their views on
uniting with Methodists, the Synod members were united
in accepting the 'Series 2' order for Holy Communion –
a modest essay in liturgical revision produced in 1967 and
retaining the ethos and language of the Book of Common
Prayer. They were asked to remain kneeling for the
entrance and departure of the senior dignitaries, en-
joined to remain in their seats until directed to the Communion rail by the stewards and informed that there
would be no collection. The keynote was restraint and
there could be no doubting that this was the Church of
England at prayer.

Wild excesses would certainly have seemed out of
place in St. Margaret's, Westminster. Since 1614 this
parish church has been the official church of the House
of Commons. The present rector, like many of his predecessors, is chaplain to the Speaker. In the time of Oliver
Cromwell members of Parliament were required to receive Holy Communion at St. Margaret's before taking
their seats in the Commons. At the end of World War II,
Winston Churchill led MPs into the church for a

spontaneous act of thanksgiving. The Lord Chancellor of England is still a regular worshipper there and follows in the footsteps of many famous figures in English history who have occupied places in a church which, although overshadowed, architecturally, by Westminster Abbey, symbolizes in a powerful way the long-standing link between the Church of England and the national corridors of power.

But the symbol has less substance now than at any other time in its history. The seats occupied by members of the General Synod are but rarely filled on Sundays. Within the past 25 years the congregation has dwindled to a point at which the weekly offerings are barely enough to cover the cost of employing a choir to lead the worship. Secularization has taken its toll in Westminster, as elsewhere, but the effects of social change have been more dramatic. No longer do the wealthy and aristocratic members of English society spend their weekends in Central London; Friday afternoon sees them on their way to country and coastal retreats, leaving churches like St. Margaret's stranded as if by a receding tide. Those who remain behind could easily be accommodated in Westminster Abbey, not 50 yards away, where they would be offered almost identical music and, frequently, the same preacher.

History and tradition combine to make so simple a suggestion quite impossible, even outrageous. Nor is the case strengthened in the slightest degree by the hard fact that a not particularly beautiful building requires an expenditure of £250,000 to repair the ravages of time. Significantly, the House of Commons no longer feels moved to come to the rescue of its own church and both Labour and Conservative administrations have indicated their unwillingness to make any financial provision for the restoraton of the building. Ceremony and tradition can be preserved, but not if they prove costly.

At this point the Church of England's survival instinct is activated. Under a scheme approved by church and state during the summer of 1972, St. Margaret's ceased to be a parish church within the diocese of London and became part of the royal peculiar which is Westminster

Abbey. Previously, the Abbey accepted no responsibility for the church on its doorstep, since it lay beyond the Dean and Chapter's jurisdiction, but now that St. Margaret's is under Abbey control the money-raising efforts of the rector and his small congregation can, if necessary, be augmented by the proceeds of national appeals for funds, one of which now seems imminent. The future of St. Margaret's is therefore quite secure and is likely to remain secure even if attendance and usefulness decline to a point at which the building is even more manifestly redundant than at present.

From this anomalous – and typically Church of England – situation, the members of the General Synod moved across Dean's Yard to the magnificent assembly hall of Church House (the finest meeting place in London) to make a decision about the most important issue to face their church in the present century. Before the debate and voting on Anglican-Methodist unity it was, however, necessary to consider a proposal that the Church of England should enter into full communion with the united churches of North India and Pakistan. These churches, which include former Anglicans and former Methodists, as well as participants from other churches, were inaugurated in 1971 as the result of a scheme markedly similar to that proposed for the uniting of Anglicans and Methodists in England. Before the Church of England could enter into full communion with them it would have to acknowledge that they were an authentic part of the Catholic Church of Christ and that their ordained ministers were part of the recognized apostolic order.

This debate, intended as a warm up for the main business, was brief. A few speakers expressed anxiety about the new churches, but there were overwhelming majorities in favour of entering into full communion with them. The voting was:

> Bishops— 36 for, 0 against
> Clergy —182 for, 5 against, 24 abstentions
> Laity —171 for, 1 against, 15 abstentions

Anyone observing the scene for the first time, after carefully studying the relevant documents, might well have concluded that the second debate would be a mere formality and the result a foregone conclusion. Which in fact it turned out to be, but not in ways dictated by rationality.

The Archbishop of Canterbury opened the debate with a memorable speech which expressed his own deep commitment to the unity scheme. Noting that the Methodist Church had already said 'Yes' to the proposals, Dr. Ramsey went on: 'If half a century ago this possibility had been forecast it would have sounded quite remarkable; and it would have sounded yet more remarkable if it had been forecast that a Methodist "Yes" would be followed by a Church of England "No".' The Archbishop then turned to examine the five main objections lodged by opponents of the scheme. His approach was that of an academic weighing arguments and seeking a result which would satisfy intellectual integrity. Fifteen minutes later the case against the scheme had, at the intellectual level, been completely demolished.

Those who were anxious about the integrity of the proposed Service of Reconciliation were asked by the Archbishop to explain why a procedure which they regarded as acceptable for the Church of North India was 'unsound' or 'immoral' in England: 'What sort of a God is it who was willing and able to answer the prayer with laying on of hands in the North India scheme but is not willing or able to answer the prayer in the Anglican-Methodist service?' Others who believed that the scheme would damage the prospects of unity between Anglicans and Roman Catholics were informed that neither the Anglican nor the Roman Catholic chairman of the Anglican-Roman Catholic International Commission shared their belief.

Dr. Ramsey next turned to those who thought the Anglican-Methodist scheme should be abandoned in favour of a multi-lateral scheme involving the other British churches. He did not believe there would be greater support for such a scheme than there was for the present proposal which had, after all, been suggested by the Church of England in the first place. Reflection on the

Church of England's initiative caused the Archbishop
momentarily to bare his teeth: 'The analogy of a bride-
groom jilting a bride at the altar is more unkind than
untrue.' Next, he discussed the position of those who
advocated local unity schemes in preference to national
schemes involving denominational structures. Here he was
sympathetic but could not believe that the rejection of
the Anglican-Methodist proposals would advance local
unity.

The remaining objection concerned the divisive effect
of acceptance upon the Church of England itself. What
would happen to the 5,000 clergymen who said in 1968
that they would not take part in the Service of Reconciliation, and the many lay people who were opposed to the
scheme? Here the Primate reminded the Synod of the
lessons of history which indicated that dissentients rarely
left the Church of England when a vote went against
them. Since those opposing the scheme did so for a great
variety of reasons he did not believe they would find
common ground as non-jurors. His final words were: 'My
prayer has been that by saying "Yes" the Synod will say
to the Methodists, our brothers in faith and our cousins
in church history, "Yes. You said you would go with us
in this way. And now we say Yes, we will go with you".'

As the Archbishop sat down to tumultuous applause,
it seemed reasonable to believe that he might, by a miracle
of grace, have managed to raise the level of discussion
far above the level to which it had fallen since the proposals were rejected by the Church Assembly in 1969,
and that, even if the required majority were not reached,
the day would be one of responsible debate. In fact, there
was no real debate. There were many speeches in favour
of the scheme. The one artisan member of the Synod
declared that he had changed his position from opposition
to support. The Bishop of Ripon led for the opposition
but could only raise points which had been effectively
demolished by Dr. Ramsey. The Bishop of Peterborough,
apparently forgetful of the fact that the Lambeth Conference of 1968 had pressed the Church of England to
accept the scheme, thought that a positive vote would
disrupt the entire Anglican Communion; in any case he

preferred federal rather than organic unity. During five hours of debate no serious attempt was made to explain opposition to the scheme in terms approximating to those introduced by Archbishop Ramsey. Yet, when the moment of decision arrived, 35 per cent of those present went through the door of the 'Noe' lobby, and so a scheme which had occupied some of the best minds of the two churches for more than a decade and which, in spite of obvious weakness and limitations, offered the possibility of new beginnings at national and local church levels, was lost for ever.

The decision revealed – or rather confirmed – two significant facts about the Church of England in 1972. First, the existence within the church of a considerable body of people opposed to change. The Archbishop of Canterbury and many of the leaders of other churches, who had listened to the debate from the public gallery, expressed surprise afterwards that a case against the unity scheme had not been stated. But opposition was not grounded primarily in the realm of the rational. It was chiefly emotional and derived its strength from deep fear of what unity with the Methodist Church would do to the established customs of the Church of England. The opponents discerned, rightly, that things could never be the same again if the two institutions were brought together. Not surprisingly, in the climate of the times, they could not say so in as many words; hence their deafening silence in the debate, but their decisive footsteps at the division. It was left to the then Bishop of Peterborough to let the cat out of the bag in the June issue of his diocesan newsletter where he wrote about the decision: 'Certainly many people will be disappointed, but with equal certainty a great many people will be relieved and reassured in that the Church of England will preserve its basic character and its apostolic order and will not face disruption and profound uncertainties about the future.'

Equally significant was the appearance – or rather the reappearance – of division within the church. Since the Reformation the Church of England has held within its ranks people whose approach to the Christian faith is from diverse angles. The explanation is to be found in

the fact that the Elizabethan settlement was primarily a
political act. There were of course theological overtones
– the Reformation in England was not unrelated to the
great theological movement which swept through Europe
in the 16th and 17th centuries – but, unlike the other
churches of the Reformation, the Church of England has
no basic confession of faith which it imposes upon its
members. The 39 Articles of Religion, now seen as a
monument to the past rather than as a document of the
present, have never been subscribed to by the laity. The
only doctrinal standards are those provided by the Catholic creeds and the forms of worship contained in the Book
of Common Prayer – all of which are patient of extremely
wide interpretation. Hence the existence in the Church
of England of different groups, held together by loyalty
to the essential Englishness of the church, expressed in
its comprehensiveness, love of freedom and pragmatic
approach to human problems.

It is quite easy to condemn such a church on the
grounds that it breeds woolliness, lack of deep conviction and considerable anarchy. Yet if it is believed that
the Christian mystery will always be apprehended differ-
ently by those who approach it and can never be fully
expressed in doctrinal statements, and if, further, it is
believed that individuals must be allowed a wide measure
of freedom in the expression of their convictions, then it
is hard to see how a united church can be so very different from the present ethos and organization of the
Church of England. Comprehensiveness and freedom must
inevitably provide lodging for some strange bed-fellows
and, though this makes for administrative inconvenience
and doctrinal untidiness, it is the central claim of the
Christian faith that commitment to Christ is able to
reconcile men and women of disparate insights, cultures
and temperaments. Since Christian unity is grounded in
allegiance to a person, not to a credal statement or an
ecclesiastical organization, it is both unnecessary and
undesirable to look for uniformity of belief and practice
within the church.

Certainly there is no such uniformity in the Church
of England, nor has there ever been. Frederick von

Hügel, a devout and learned Roman Catholic, defined three abiding elements in all religion: the institutional, the intellectual and the mystical. A mature believer would doubtless hold these three elements in perfect tension, but the majority of Christians tend to stress one element at the expense of the others and the degree of interaction between the elements varies very considerably. When, however, there is a marked emphasis on one element a particular approach to the Christian faith becomes apparent and, since people of common heart and mind enjoy one another's company, it is hardly surprising if they come together in groups. Hence the existence of division between churches and within churches.

The Church of England provides a resting place for Christians who are attracted or impelled by all three elements. The great majority are most accurately defined in terms of the institutional. This may sound ominous since anything associated with institutions or the institutional is currently suspect, but von Hügel's analysis penetrated much deeper than this. He was concerned with those who have a deep feeling for the historical and value continuity with the past. They see the church as central to the Christian faith and are concerned that the life of the church shall accurately reflect the nature of the Gospel as it has been traditionally understood and transmitted across the centuries. Naturally, there is much conservatism and caution involved in such an approach, but there is also great wisdom and deep commitment to people and communities. There is no possibility of change within the Church of England unless those who approach religion in this way can be convinced that the proposals do no violence to the past and pose no threat to the continuance of the church in a recognizable, and preferably familiar, form.

Although the characteristic approach of the Church of England is pragmatic rather than doctrinaire, pastoral rather than academic, it has always greatly valued the contribution of the intellect in its quest for truth. It has always aspired to have a learned clergy, even though it has frequently been obliged to make do with bishops and priests whose academic accomplishments were

modest. From time to time it has produced scholars of
the first rank who have enjoyed international reputations.
Never has it sought to restrain any of its members who
felt moved by a spirit of enquiry to seek new truths or to
express old truths in new ways. Such enquirers are still to
be found within the Church of England. When their
discoveries lead them over the edges of the pathway of
orthodoxy they are usually dubbed 'liberals' or 'radicals'.
As is normally the case with pioneers, their immediate
influence is negligible but their long-term influence is
far-reaching and, in the end, formative. They provide the
impetus for change and though the Church of England
tolerates, and sometimes enjoys, their presence in its
ranks it causes most of them excruciating frustration by
means of neglect or promotion. If they are able to combine their intellectual pursuits with pastoral care they
are more likely to be heard; bishops and parish priests
rank higher than professors and editors.

Then there are those who respond chiefly to the mystical element in religion, expressed in ways which tran-
scend ordinary human experience. There can be no true
religion – certainly no Christian religion – which does not
include this element. But its power is more compelling for
some than for others and those who are most strongly influenced may be divided into two distinct groups. First, the
sacramentalists whose mystical experiences are expressed
in and through symbolism of various kinds. They value
church ceremonial and are specially sensitive to colour,
light, movement and certain types of music. These things
provide a doorway to the numinous and, though they
are most commonly associated with the worship of the
Roman Catholic Church, there are a significant number
of Anglicans for whom they occupy a crucial place in
religious life and experience. The size of this group has
increased very considerably during the past 100 years,
but there were 'High Church' Anglicans in the 17th
century and the mystical element in mediaeval religion
was developed to a point at which it was indistinguishable
from superstition and required the checks of history and
intellect. The second group who travel the way of mysti-
cism are the so-called evangelicals, who have little room

for symbolism but are deeply aware of a personal relationship with Christ. This relationship is uncomplicated
and has a high emotional content. It demands neither
priest nor sacrament and has a powerful effect upon the
emotions of those who establish such a relationship, or,
as they would say, are possessed by Christ. The Bible,
often regarded as verbally inspired and infallible, is for
the evangelical a constant source of insight and encouragement. He sees it as demanding a simple and restrained
style of life in which the body is regarded with considerable suspicion and amusements with something approaching fear. Personal prayer has a prominent and permanent
place on the evangelical time-table. Christians of
this approach are normally associated with churches
which have a pronounced evangelical image, but, again,
a significant number of evangelicals are to be found
within the Church of England. They trace their origins
to the Reformation, recall their immense influence on the
life of the Church of England during the first half of the
19th century and are now beginning to enjoy a new
confidence derived from a period of growth in the 1960s.

Most Anglicans glory in the comprehensiveness which
permits these three different groups to live side by side
in one church. At different periods in the history of the
Church of England one of the approaches has pre-
dominated, but the majority of Anglicans believe the life
of their church to be most healthy when the three are
held together in a more or less equal tension. Problems
arise when one or other of the groups seeks to dominate
the others and arrogate to itself exclusive control of the
church's power structure and channels of communication. During the first four decades of the present century
certain well-organized and amply financed organizations
attempted to do just this on behalf of the high church
(Anglo-catholic) and low church (Evangelical) groups.
The results were not edifying. Partisanship and bitterness
occupied positions in the life of the Church of England at
every level which seemed out of place in a body claiming
to be Christian.

When the Church of England began to reconstruct its
life in 1945, it appeared that the war years had served

one useful purpose by cleansing the church of party
strife. Parishes of different traditions no longer devoted
their energies to internecine warfare. It was possible to
attend the councils of the church without having to
endure partisan confrontation. The societies and trusts
which promoted particular points of view were weak and
largely ignored. For a period of twenty years it was not
unreasonable to suggest that the days of the 'parties'
were ended. All had become good, middle-of-the-road
Anglicans. There were, however, embers of partisanship
waiting for a cause to fan them into a blaze, and, para-
doxically, this was provided by the movement towards
Christian unity which developed a new sense of urgency
after a Faith and Order Conference held in Nottingham
in 1964.

Conversations between the Church of England and the
Methodist Church began in 1956 and were conducted at
a leisurely pace until a preliminary report was published
in 1963. This report aroused little interest in either church
and quickly went out of print. By 1965, however, the
joint commission responsible for the conversations was
in a position to make specific proposals for uniting the
two churches and it was at this point that the Anglo-
Catholic and Evangelical sparks began to fly. The two
groups were opposed to the unity scheme for diametri-
cally opposed reasons, but they found common cause in
their opposition to proposals which the joint commission
had carefully engineered in the hope of securing broad
support from both churches. Anglo-Catholic and Evangelical spokesmen toured the country fostering opposition,
while those aligned to the institutional and intellectual
elements in the Church of England were happy to
support the scheme. When the Church Assembly voted
in 1969, party warfare was too fierce to be ignored and
the elections for the new General Synod in 1970 were, in
most dioceses, fought on a party basis. In the end, the
coalition of Anglo-catholic and Evangelical opponents of
the Anglican-Methodist unity scheme – described by one
distinguished Free Church leader as the strangest alliance
since that of Pontius Pilate and King Herod – proved
lethal and the wishes of the majority were frustrated. A

quest for unity had served only to promote division.

By the evening of 3 May, 1972 it was therefore possible to see the Church of England as an institution which had once occupied a central position in the life of the English people but was now relegated to the periphery of English society. Many of its privileges remained, but its influence had declined to a point lower than anything experienced since England became a Christian nation. Faced with the need to adjust its life to a new situation, and still endowed with considerable resources, the Church of England was saddled with the burdens of conservatism and division, which made significant progress painfully slow, if not actually impossible.

In these circumstances, it was hardly surprising that the Archbishop of Canterbury and other perceptive members of the General Synod returned to their dioceses worried men. The day's events had confirmed their worst fears. No longer could the crisis in the Church of England be overlooked or dismissed as a temporary condition. Its roots ran deep and only a fool would be allowed the luxury of believing that the crisis could easily or quickly be overcome. Dr. Ramsey commented: 'We are in darkness, we must become more humble.'

chapter 2

People and Property

Humility has not hitherto been one of the most prominent hall-marks of the Church of England. Not that it has ever made such extravagant claims for itself as the Church of Rome, or wielded such power over men and nations. Like so many English institutions, its arrogance has been of the silent sort: expressed not so much by what it says and does but mainly by what it takes for granted.

History has not been helpful at this point. The Church of England pre-dates the organization of the state. Throughout the Middle Ages church and state were inextricably bound together. In north-east England the prince bishops of Durham owned five castles, raised their own armies, minted their own money, and provided a convenient buffer against the marauding Scots. Nowhere is the privileged position of the Church of England more clearly visible than at a Coronation. The king or queen is anointed and crowned by the Archbishop of Canterbury. In recent years representatives of other churches have been permitted minor roles in the ceremony, but the occasion is pre-eminently one in which the Church of England exercises its traditional authority in the life of the nation.

Another sign of privilege is to be found in the presence of 26 of the 43 diocesan bishops in the House of Lords. They are in Parliament not because it is anticipated that they will make a useful contribution to the legislative process – though in fact many of the present bishops do – but because the leaders of the Church of England have for many centuries been identified with the centre of political power. The prayers which begin the daily sittings of the House of Commons are conducted by the

Speaker's chaplain who, irrespective of the religious
allegiance of the Speaker, is always a priest of the Church
of England. Move away from London to the provinces
and no county occasion is complete without the presence of an Anglican bishop. In spite of secularization,
bishops of the Established Church are still privileged and
influential, and this is particularly true of the occupants
of ancient dioceses. Soon after his translation from
Southwark (founded in 1905) to Winchester (founded in
705), Bishop Cyril Garbett commented on the different
atmosphere in which he found himself working. Whereas
the majority of people living in South London neither
knew nor cared whether they had a bishop, the population
of Hampshire were extremely conscious of the place
occupied by the Bishop of Winchester in their community life. The tradition built up over twelve centuries
offered the bishop a position of privilege and influence.

A similar situation is encountered in the majority of
provincial towns and villages where some semblance of
community life remains. The vicar of an ancient parish
church (of which there are more than 8,000 in England)
is accorded a status which will never be enjoyed by the
local Roman Catholic priest or Free Church minister,
be they never so gifted and friendly. In many places he
will automatically assume the chairmanship of committees and governing bodies of one kind or another.

While it would be a serious mistake to over-estimate
the influence which these privileged positions afford, it
would be equally mistaken to write them off as insignificant. They are clear evidence of the marriage of church
and state which has characterized English history for
more than a thousand years and which has not yet come
to an end, even though it has in practice been greatly
modified.

Whatever the effect of the marriage has been upon the
life of the English nation as a whole – good men are
divided on the matter – it cannot be denied that the
effect upon the Church of England has been to link it
permanently with the most privileged sector of English
society. The Established Church is, not surprisingly, part
of 'the establishment', and the results of this are clear

for all to see when the membership of the Church of England is subjected to close scrutiny.

The Paul Report[1] included the results of some fascinating research into the educational and social background of diocesan bishops during the period 1860–1960 carried out by David H. J. Morgan. This indicated that every diocesan bishop in office in 1960 had attended a public school, as indeed had all but a handful of their predecessors during the previous 100 years. Only five of the 43 had attended universities other than Oxford and Cambridge. Some tentative figures about the social background of the bishops suggested that just over half had connexions with the landed gentry or the peerage. This pattern has been maintained over the past twelve years.

Leslie Paul also included in his report the results of an enquiry into the backgrounds of men training for ordination in 1962 carried out by Anthony P. M. Coxon.[2] This showed that no fewer than 35 per cent had attended public or independent schools while a further 43 per cent had attended grammar and high schools. Only 22 per cent came from secondary modern or similar schools. 67 per cent described themselves as middle-class, 1.2 per cent said they were upper-class, and 29 per cent were related to Church of England clergymen. Given this background it is hardly surprising that the clerical leadership of the Church of England reflects with unnerving accuracy the attitudes and assumptions of the middle classes, and it is necessary to place only one foot inside an episcopal palace or a vicarage to receive confirmation of this fact.

An examination of the membership of the General Synod reveals a similar story. While it is no longer quite accurate to describe the House of Laity as 'the squires from the shires and the spinsters from the spas', twelve of its 251 members are titled, 17 are retired service officers, 13 are the wives of clergymen. The chairman of the Central Board of Finance is a KCB and a KBE, and the deputy vice-chairman is a retired naval captain. The chairman of the Missionary and Ecumenical Council is

[1] *The Deployment and Payment of the Clergy* by Leslie Paul, Church Information Office, 1964, p. 282ff.
[2] *ibid*. p. 280ff.

an earl and the chairman of the Pensions Board a KCVO. The lay members of the Synod's panel of chairmen are a knight, a bishop's daughter and a professor. Public school and professional backgrounds predominate, and the one identifiable artisan member – an East London fire-brigade worker – is something of a curiosity.

The privileged character of those who comprise the Church of England's leadership is not of course to be seen as a criticism of the middle and upper classes. They are simply performing one of their traditional roles in English society, and the Church of England, like many other institutions, leans heavily upon their skills and sense of responsibility. But when a branch of the Christian church has a membership which is drawn almost exclusively from the more privileged members of society certain questions have to be raised. It is not only the bishops and the priests and the members of the General Synod who come from the middle classes; the overwhelming majority of the ordinary church members have the same position in English society. Hence the relative ease with which the Church of England functions in predominantly middle-class communities and the desperate struggle to survive which characterizes its life in artisan areas. This is not a new situation, nor is it a problem facing only the Church of England, as Charles Booth indicated in 1904:

The great section of the population, which passes by the name of the working classes, lying socially between the lower middle class and the 'poor', remains, as a whole, outside of all religious bodies, whether organised as churches or as missions; and as those of them who do join any church become almost indistinguishable from the class with which they then mix, the change that has really come about is not so much *of* as *out* of the class to which they have belonged.[3]

A similar story concerning the Roman Catholic Church in France is told by Canon Boulard in his classic study of Mass attendance in France from 1830–1956.[4]

[3] *Life and Labour of the People in London,* 3rd Series by C. Booth VII p. 399, Methuen, 1902.
[4] *An Introduction to Religious Sociology* by F. Boulard, Darton Longman & Todd, 1960.

These are uncomfortable facts for any church which is constantly reminded by its reading of the New Testament that Jesus of Nazareth had a special concern for the underprivileged members of society and, indeed, declared that his message was particularly directed towards their liberation. The comfortably-off people in Jewish society came under his condemnation and were told, bluntly, that it was easier for a rich man to pass through the eye of a needle than it was for him to enter the kingdom of heaven. There is more than a hint in the New Testament that 'the poor man of Nazareth' was concerned to bring about a radical change in the structure of society, and so there is something decidedly odd about a situation in which companies of well-heeled and influential people assemble in churches to sing 'He hath put down the mighty from their seat, and hath exalted the humble and meek'.

The point has now been reached where the middle-class character of the Church of England has become a major obstacle to this church ever again becoming the church of the English people as a whole. Members of the artisan class, who still constitute the overwhelming majority of the population of England, find themselves in a strange – even alien – atmosphere when they enter a parish church. No matter how carefully and imaginatively the worship is ordered, it takes for granted middle class attitudes and assumptions. Styles of dress, modes of greeting (where such liberties are permitted), accents in speech and a heavy emphasis on verbal communication combine to produce a community in which few artisans can feel at home. A comparison between a Sunday morning liturgy in a parish church and a Friday evening 'liturgy' in a backstreet pub or a Saturday afternoon 'liturgy' in a football stadium may well invite theological confusion, but it is illuminating for any who are concerned to discover why working-class people feel ill at ease when they join the Church of England at prayer. Nor is the problem solved when alert and friendly congregations meet in informal small groups in the homes of their members. In many ways it becomes more acute since a bricklayer feels even less comfortable in the home of a bank manager or a university lecturer than he does in the institutional atmosphere of a parish church. The question to be faced is whether it is possible to become an active member of the Church of England without first undergoing conversion to middle class standards and attitudes? The nature of the Christian faith will not permit the church to answer 'No', but honesty will not allow it to answer 'Yes'.

There is a further problem arising from the class structure of the church and this concerns the extent to which middle class attitudes have isolated the Church of England from the social revolution which has been taking place during the greater part of the present century. Traditional middle class assumptions about the nature of leadership and methods of education are no longer acceptable in contemporary society. The fact that a man or woman has attended a 'good' school or graduated at Oxbridge does not justify assumptions of leadership or superior knowledge. Paternalism is out; equality and participation are in. But the Church of England has yet to recognize this. Its traditional assumptions of superiority and dominance are maintained, if not actually reinforced, by the middle class ethos in which it now operates. Bishops are expected to travel in style, with pennants or coats of arms on their cars. The system which rewards certain clergymen with appointments to honorary cathedral canonries (for reasons known only to the bishop who makes the appointment) has yet to be seriously challenged, nor will it while congregations continue to rejoice when their vicar is so rewarded. The orders of precedence produced by many cathedrals extend far beyond the demands of decency and order to a carefully calculated hierarchical pecking order not unlike that of a royal court. None of these things is important in itself, but taken together they reflect certain attitudes to life and to the church, and the fact that few people within the church pause to wonder whether they are really compatible with the central meaning of the Christian Gospel is highly significant. It is also extremely dangerous, since many thoughtful people outside the church asked the questions a long time ago and, failing to obtain

a satisfactory answer, decided that the church could not
be regarded as a credible instrument of the faith preached
by Jesus of Nazareth: 'I am among you as one who
serves'.

Another factor militating against humility is the
Church of England's size and strength. There is much
talk about the decline of the Church of England, and a
later chapter will discuss some recent trends, but weakness is relative rather than absolute and, in spite of
serious losses during the present century, very considerable resources of manpower, money and buildings remain.
Commenting on this in his report, Leslie Paul said, 'Viewed
religiously the number of worshippers may be held to be
unsatisfactory, but considered socially it is formidable,
and makes the Church of England by far and away the
most important social institution in the land. . . . It
reaches a larger group than any other voluntary organization which depends for its existence upon the regular
attendance of its members at a place of meeting, their
participation in a variety of voluntary activities and their
voluntary contributions. No political party commands
such a weekly "audience" or has the services of so large a
professional body. The church is only surpassed in
audience figures by the organs of mass communication –
the press, television and radio.'[5]

Among the more useful developments in the Church of
England since 1945 has been the establishment of a
statistical unit which now publishes regular reports of
significant facts and figures concerning the life of the
church. Unfortunately, these reports, compiled at considerable expense and at the price of much grumbling
from the parochial clergy who are asked to provide local
statistics, have never become the basis of serious study,
much less strategic planning, but they do provide facts
rather than fantasies for those who are concerned about
the numerical strength of the church and changes in
patterns of support for its institutional life.[6]

On 31 December 1969, the Church of England had

[5] *ibid*, p. 26f.
[6] The figures which follow are taken from *The Church of England
Year Book 1971–72*, Church Information Office, 1971.

11,162 parishes. Of these, 15 have populations of over 30,000 but the majority (7,714) have under 5,000 people. Almost one-third (3,624) are under 1,000. This parochial network provides the church with a means of contact with the entire population of the country. No one is outside the network and most people are within easy walking distance of the building which is the base of the church's activities in their locality. There are 17,681 buildings in which regular worship is offered. More than 8,000 of these are mediaeval structures of considerable beauty and historic interest. They are nearly always the oldest building in a community, occupy a prominent position and, over many generations, have attracted the attendance of parishioners, if not for regular worship at least at the key moments of birth, marriage and death. The repair and upkeep of the buildings, whether ancient, Victorian or modern, is now one of the Church of England's major problems but this fact, and recent questioning of the basis of the parochial system, should not lead to an undervaluing of an arrangement which provides the church with a recognizable base in every community in the land. Many other organizations – political, social and commercial – would count themselves singularly fortunate to be endowed with so comprehensive a network for their activities.

The parishes are divided between 43 dioceses, each of which has at least one bishop, who is responsible for the overall supervision and direction of the church's activities in the area, and also a cathedral, normally staffed by priests with specialist functions. The parishes themselves are served by 13,522 full time clergymen, the overwhelming majority of whom reside in close proximity to a church building, and a further 4,680 clergymen are serving as chaplains, teachers, priest-workers or on a part-time basis in retirement. In other words, the Church of England has more than 18,000 professionally-trained priests at work throughout the country. The activities of these men are augmented by 1,136 full and part-time layworkers, 6,424 voluntary, but trained, readers, and 1,882 lay members of Religious Communities. As in other walks of life, these servants of the church vary in their effectiveness but the strength of an organization that can keep so many trained representatives in the field ought not to be underestimated.

As a 'folk church', to which the entire population of the country has traditionally belonged except when individuals have opted out, it is not easy to calculate the active membership of the Church of England and the various yardsticks employed can all be criticized in some way or other. Baptism figures are not very helpful since it is still the custom for this sacrament to be administered to infants, the majority of whom do not enter into any living relationship with the church community. It may be noted in passing, however, that on 30 June 1968 some 27,756,000 (nearly 60 per cent) of the total population of England had been baptized in the Church of England. During 1968, 381,447 infants and 8,602 adults were baptized at Anglican fonts. Confirmation is a slightly more reliable guide in that it involves a conscious decision on the part of the individuals concerned, following a period of preparatory training, but here again figures need careful handling since many of the adolescents who are presented for Confirmation do not remain in active church membership. The number of Confirmed members of the Church of England at 30 June 1968 was 9,691,000.

A more realistic picture emerges when consideration is given to electoral rolls and numbers of communicants at the great festivals of the church. Once again, certain reservations must be made: some of those who in a now distant past had their names entered on a parish electoral roll are no longer active in the life of the church; a proportion of those who attend church at Christmas and Easter are not seen very often during the rest of the year and their contribution to the church's life may be minimal. Even so, there were 2,636,412 people on electoral rolls at the end of 1968. During the same year 1,974,844 people received Holy Communion at Easter, and 1,788,935 at Christmas. As a proportion of the total population of the country, these figures are far from impressive, but they represent nonetheless a quite size-able constituency. When every allowance has been made for convention, superstition, nostalgia, sentiment and all

those other factors which take people into churches, an
expressed allegiance of just under 2 millions cannot
lightly be dismissed as insignificant. Nor can the 1,605,670
people who formed the usual congregation every
Sunday in 1968. They constitute the solid rock of Church
of England membership and play an important part
in whatever life and witness is offered by the local
churches.

Figures relating to the income of parish churches also
present a substantial picture. The total incomes of parochial church councils in 1968 amounted to £34,558,141,
an increase of almost £1 million over the total income in
1966. A local church's income is derived from many
different sources – collections, subscriptions, gift days,
bazaars and, in a few fortunate places, dividends and
rents – but the bulk of it comes from the pockets and
purses of those whose concern for the church is strong
enough to make they give a regular contribution to its
funds. Again, a company of people whose interest in an
institution leads them to provide over £34½ millions for
its work in a 12-month period deserves to be taken
seriously. Those who are opposed to the church's work or
are scornful of its efforts are far less successful in raising
money to support their own viewpoints and organizations.
Nor are they noticeably more generous in their handling
of money. Of the £34½ millions raised by parochial
church councils in 1968, approximately £6½ millions were
given to causes – ecclesiastical and charitable – outside
the parishes. Approximately £8¾ millions went to the
payment of stipends to clergy and other full-time church
workers. Nearly £6 millions went on the maintenance
and upkeep of church buildings, £8½ millions on capital
projects and almost £750,000 on educational work.
During the same year, the income of the Church Commissioners amounted to a record total of £21,889,356
and 65 per cent of this helped to provide stipends for the
clergy.

These figures need to be remembered in any discussion
of the Church of England's present position and its
future. Whatever the weaknesses and absurdities discernible in the life of the church – and there is no shortage of

either at any level – it remains a major English institution. No useful purpose is served by supposing that it is now so small as to be insignificant or that it is likely to disappear during the next decade. There is growing evidence that the Church of England has now entered a period of steep decline, the long-term consequences of which could be extremely serious, but, even so, there remain very substantial reserves of support and institutional capital which demand that the current debate must concentrate on a church which is not going to disappear overnight.

Unlike the churches of continental Europe, the Church of England has but rarely aroused the hostility of significant sections of the nation. There were occasions during the early years of the 19th century when bishops were jeered while on their way to the House of Lords, and dead cats were hurled into their carriages. But, for the most part, the Church of England has been accepted as a normal part of the English scene. Frequently it has been ignored, except on occasions of community or personal crisis, but never has it been persecuted. As a result it has, in a variety of subtle ways, remained intertwined in the fabric of the national life.

Any attempt to assess the influence of this large and ancient institution is bound to run into insuperable difficulties. A great deal of what the church stands for and exists to promote is intangible. It concerns the deep things of human personality and the hidden influences which go into the making of community. If the 11,162 parishes were areas marked out for the sale of, say, instant coffee, with the 17,681 churches serving as warehouses and the 18,000 clergymen functioning as retailers or representatives, it would be quite easy to calculate, on a weekly basis, the influence and profitability of the organization. But the church does not exist to sell anything; its task is to express values. Perhaps the best way to calculate the effectiveness of the church would be to take two identical communities, one of which had an active Christian congregation and the other no Christian group at all. Over a period of 50 years these communities could be closely observed and at the end of the period an

assessment made of any differences which were notice-
able between them. This would be an interesting exercise
but, here again, the results would have to be treated with
extreme caution. Communities are never identical. The
way in which human beings react – individually or cor-
porately – to particular events and stimuli varies very
considerably indeed. If, for example, the community
which had a Christian congregation turned out to be
the happier and more integrated place, this would not
necessarily be due to the influence of the church. Certain
other factors, equally difficult to isolate and quantify,
might offer a better explanation. The same is true of
individuals. Does it make any difference whether or not
I go to church? is an unanswerable question when
couched in general terms. For some people the answer
is a clear 'Yes', for others a clear 'No', but for many
there is no clear answer – only a feeling that association
with the church is in some indefinable way meaningful
and helpful.

In spite of all these obvious difficulties, an attempt
must now be made to assess the value of certain activities
of the Church of England which are, in part, observable
and which represent a valid expression of the convictions which brought the church into being and motivate
its most active members. Once again, there are dangers
in generalization. Parishes vary considerably and many
different factors contribute to the unevenness of performance. In some places the leadership of the clergy is
decisive; in others a haloed saint would scarcely make a
difference. The history and the geography of a particular
community is far more influential than is generally
recognized; a church with a long history of identification
with a community which has a recognizable shape, say,
a small country town, will function with much greater
ease than a church of Victorian foundation which stands
in the decaying back-streets of an impersonal industrial
town. Failure to take account of these factors, which
normally have a dramatic effect on the life of a local
church, has so far frustrated all attempts to reform the
parochial system in order to meet the needs of urban,
rather than rural, communities.

B

For the purpose of this assessment, an 'average' parish will be assumed. It has a population of about 3,000, is served by one priest, has a 14th century building, stands on the edge of a fairly large town and, in addition to middle-class housing, has a small estate of council houses. An observer of this scene will notice three types of activity taking place in and from the parish church. There is the personal, pastoral ministry of the vicar. He is a university graduate and now in his early 50s, having worked as a parish priest for the past 25 years. Part of his day is spent in the vicarage study, most afternoons are devoted to visiting the homes of parishioners. In any week, several people will call to see him to discuss personal problems or needs, and other conversations will take place during the course of his visiting. A fair proportion of those who discuss their problems with the priest will have only a tenuous connection with the church and may enter the church building only for baptisms, marriages and funerals. Marital and family problems are the most common reasons for consultation, and a certain number of those who call have psychiatric disorders of some kind; the majority will be women. They make use of the vicar in this way because he may be presumed to have a sympathetic ear, a certain amount of experience of human problems and time to give to individuals. These assets combine to make a very useful combination. Not every medical practitioner is skilled in handling non-physical problems, most of them are exceedingly busy and can devote only a limited amount of time to individual patients. Professional social workers are still few and far between in most areas of Britain, they operate from 'official' and often impersonal premises, and, because they are still fairly new on the scene, are not yet established in the confidence of everyone needing help. The vicar is, therefore, able to perform a certain function in the community. Some parishioners will find their encounters with him more helpful than others do, and the proportion of people in the neighbourhood who use him in this way will always be quite small. But the Church of England is, through its clergy, making a contribution of this kind to the life of over 11,000 communities. Opinions as to the usefulness of this contribution may vary; it can hardly be ignored in any objective assessment of the church's influence on English society.

The parish church and its ancillary buildings will provide activities for about 100 adults and the same number of children. Most of them will share in regular acts of worship, the majority of the children will be involved in some form of educational activity, and up to half of the adults will belong to a group, ranging from the parochial church council, which is concerned with the organization of church life in the parish, to a young wives' fellowship which offers social activities to a particular section of the community. Since it is impossible to calculate the effect of worship and prayer upon those who take part in church services, this element in the parish church's work must be left on one side, notwithstanding the belief of most Christians that this is the most important aspect of the life of the Christian community. But it is impossible to ignore the fact that the church provides a setting in which a certain number of people can find acceptance and experience a sense of belonging. The church is not alone in this. Townswomen's guilds, parent-teacher associations, sports clubs, public houses and many other formal and informal groups offer similar experiences of acceptance and community to different people in every locality. They are part of the fabric of English society. Without them the life of the nation and of innumerable individuals would be impoverished. Hence the importance of an organization which provides 17,681 centres of community in every part of the country, from the remotest hamlet to London's Trafalgar Square.

If the parish churches did no more than provide experiences of acceptance and belonging to the 1,605,670 people who attend them every Sunday, they would be performing a significant function. In fact, their influence is much wider, since the church is committed to involvement in the life of the community as a whole. From every parish church, individuals and groups go out to share some of their insights with others and to express their beliefs in practical action. The vicar is not the only member of the church who serves as counsellor and friend to those in trouble. It is rare to find a congregation which does not include two or three people who are known and trusted in the neighbourhood and are constantly being called upon to listen to the problems of individuals and to give help to people in need. Members of an 'average' parish church are among the first to be called upon to lend a hand with any community effort. It may be a flag day for a charity, the collection of signatures for a petition, the organization of an outing for elderly people, the reclamation of waste land for a children's playground, or any one of that multitude of activities which a living community undertakes for the enhancement of its life. Those who attend churches are accustomed to being called hypocrites; they are also used to being called upon for help when the number of volunteers from other quarters is limited.

In each of these three ways, the Church of England makes a contribution to the life of the nation. They have been briefly described here because the crisis in which the church is now engulfed often causes them to be overlooked. There is much in the life of the Church of England which calls for criticism and there is ample cause for alarm about its future, but there is also solid achievement and self-sacrificing service which neither conservatism nor incompetence has, so far, been able to destroy. A good deal of the frustration among those who are now concerned for the reform and renewal of the Church of England derives from a clear recognition of how much better the present pattern of its work could be carried out if certain elements in the ecclesiastical machine were modified. Given the vast resources of the Church of England, the potential for significant and influential work is infinitely greater than the present accomplishments. And this work will always be centred primarily in the parishes – however widely the traditional concept is reinterpreted in the light of current social trends – because this is where people are and the church exists for the sake of people. Reformers believe that the clergy can be freed for more and better pastoral work. They believe that the community life of local churches can be strengthened and made more effective. They believe that the church can make a much more substantial contribution to the life of the nation as a whole.

Underlying the pressure for change there is a deep faith in the insights and power of the Christian gospel, and a burning conviction that the church is one of the important means by which these insights and this power are expressed. The reformer is concerned for change because he believes that the Church of England, which has made a massive contribution to the life of England in the past, can make an equally significant, though very different, contribution in the future. The way forward is by taking the church's past extremely seriously, and by taking its present and future even more seriously. Like a human body, the church has a delicate structure which is the result of evolution over many centuries and a variety of subtle influences. Major surgery may well be called for if parts of the body are diseased or have decayed. But the surgeons had better treat the body with respect and with their highest skills, otherwise they may find themselves with a corpse on the operating table. At the moment there is no great danger of this, since the reformers have lost much of their old zeal and the Church of England faces the future in a mood of uncertainty and with its confidence undermined, if not actually destroyed. In many ways the ethos of the church parallels that of the nation as a whole, which is hardly surprising for the two have lived together for a very long time.

chapter 3

The Statistics of Decline

The low morale of the Church of England is directly related to the falling away of support which has characterized the whole of the 20th century and become even more marked during the past decade. Commenting on his eight years as rector of Woolwich, Nicolas Stacey said, in his admirably frank autobiography: 'Ours was probably one of the most "successful" Anglican churches in working-class riverside London. But our achievement was that in four and a half years the regular members of the congregation had increased from about fifty to 100 mostly drawn from socially superior areas outside our parish. Yet if each priest from our staff had persuaded ten new people each year to join the worshipping community we should have had a regular congregation of 400. As I realize now, we failed because we never had any chance of succeeding. It was naïve of me to imagine that we could have succeeded – a naïveté, let it be said, that was shared by many others in the leadership of the Church of England.'[1] Before turning to examine some of the statistics of decline, it is, however, necessary to demythologize certain beliefs about the degree of support enjoyed by the Church of England in the 19th century. That the churches of the Victorian era, particularly from 1880 to the turn of the century, nearly always had large congregations is not open to doubt. Even so, the majority of the English people did not attend church, nor had they done so since the beginning of the Industrial Revolution. A census of church attendance carried out in Sheffield in 1881 revealed that on the Sunday under survey 87,756

[1] *Who Cares* by Nicolas Stacey, p.199f, Anthony Blond, 1971.

people had attended one or other of the 196 places of worship in the city. A breakdown of these figures shows that at the morning and evening services in these churches approximately half the available seats were occupied. The population of Sheffield at that time was 284,410, so it appears that no more than one in three people were in church on an average Sunday.[2] In 1899 the Archdeacon of London admitted: 'The fact is that the population is increasing with such enormous rapidity that we are never able to overtake the neglect of 100 years ago.'[3] Three years later it was estimated that only one in five of the population of Greater London attended church. Church attendance in country districts was much higher than in the towns but it is obvious that in the majority of country towns the church buildings simply were not large enough to house more than half the population.

The present century had by its mid-point seen a dramatic falling off in church attendance in every part of England. In their survey of York, published in 1951, Rowntree and Lavers showed that the number of adults in the churches of the city on an average Sunday had fallen from 17,060 in 1901 to 10,220 in 1948. During the same period the population of York increased from 48,000 to 78,500; thus the proportion of the population in church had fallen from 35.5 per cent to 13 per cent.[4] In Sheffield the population rose from 284,410 in 1881 to just over half a million in 1956. During this time average Sunday attendance at Church of England places of worship fell from 33,835 to a figure somewhere between 12,000 and 13,000.[5] Declines of this magnitude cannot simply be shrugged off, no matter the reasons for them. They indicate a marked change of attitude on the part of a significant number of people and a different atmosphere in which an institution is required to function. It was not until the late 1950s, however, that Bishop Wickham's study of Sheffield offered unchallengeable

[2] *Church and People in an Industrial City* by E. R. Wickham, p. 148, Lutterworth Press, 1957.
[3] *Church Congress Report* (1899) p. 37.
[4] *English Life and Leisure* by B. Seebohm Rowntree and G. R. Lavers, Longman, 1951.
[5] Wickham, *op. cit.*, p. 169.

statistical evidence from one area of the country and began to ask serious questions about the Church of England's policy – or lack of it – in a time of violent change. Only a handful of sociologists, theologians and churchmen have considered Wickham's approach to be worth pursuing, and their modest efforts have earned them more brickbats than bouquets from the Church of England's leadership.

Baptism does not offer an adequate guide to church membership since the reasons which lead parents to seek this sacrament on behalf of their infant children rarely include active commitment to a local Christian community. The number of children brought to Baptism does, however, give some indication of how the population at large regard the cultic element in religion and their relationship to the church. Between 1902 and 1958 the numbers of Baptisms in the Church of England per 1,000 live births in the country declined by 12 per cent from 658 to 579. Spread over a period of more than half a century this represented a very gradual decline and, for some unascertainable reason, there was actually an increase to over 700 (717 in 1926) per 1,000 for the whole of the 1920s. The figures for the period 1958 to 1968 tell a different story. In a space of ten years, Baptisms declined by 15 per cent from 579 to 490 per 1,000 live births. The metropolitan dioceses of London and Southwark registered declines of over 30 per cent in this period. Any consideration of these figures must take account of the fact that the past 25 years have seen a growing concern about the administration of infant Baptism which has in some parishes led to stricter requirements of parents and godparents and sometimes discouragement of the practice of infant Baptism among non-churchgoing families. But this does not account for the steep drop in the number of children being presented for Baptism; the explanation is to be found in the attitude of parents who either do not give the possibility of Baptism a thought or see no point in going through a ceremony which has no meaning for them. Viewed in this light, the decline cannot in itself be taken to represent a weakening of church membership. Much more significant is the decline in the number of adults coming forward for Baptism and, presumably, active membership of the church. Between 1962 and 1968 this figure fell from 12,000 to 8,602 – a drop of nearly 30 per cent.

Although Confirmation is a long way from being an infallible index of the strength of the Church of England it can obviously be given greater weight than Baptism. The years between 1911 and 1958 saw a decline of 20 per cent in the number Confirmed. In 1911 42.8 in every 1,000 young people in the 12-20 age group were Confirmed by Anglican bishops; by 1958 it was 34 in every 1,000. This was a substantial decline but, since it was spread over nearly 50 years, was hardly noticed. The figures for the decade 1958 to 1968 are less easily overlooked: the decline was one of 37 per cent, the number of Confirmations per 1,000 young people falling from 34 to 21.4. In the diocese of Southwark the number of actual Confirmations fell from 7,038 in 1961 to 3,581 in 1968 (48.9 per cent) and, although these figures require a slight adjustment to take account of the post-war birthrate bulge, the picture they present is clear enough. This picture is also reflected to a certain extent in the numbers of children attending Church of England Sunday Schools. The decline during the seven years between 1953 and 1960 was almost equal to the decline (27 per cent) during the previous 50 years. In 1901, 301 children in every 1,000 in the 3-14 age group attended Sunday School; by 1960 this had fallen to 133. Once again, an allowance must be made for changes in the Church of England's approach to education and initiation. Confirmation courses have become more exacting in terms of their length and content. The enthusiasm for children's work which characterized the late-Victorian era has largely evaporated as a result of experience which indicates that the influence of the church upon children whose parents are not involved in its life is meagre. But, when every allowance has been made, it is necessary to recognize that these statistics of decline represent a trend never before experienced by the Church of England. The novelty of the situation may, perhaps, explain the current lack of concern. It is possible that the figures – and their implications – have induced the immobility that sometimes accompanies fear. Whatever the explanation, there is as yet no indication that the Church of England as a whole is ready to grapple with these figures in an effort to discover their meaning and message. Simply to rehearse the statistics is to invite accusations of pessimism or 'rocking the boat'.

The interests of accuracy and reality demand, however, that this risk shall be taken. Now it is the turn of the figures relating to Communicants at the Christmas and Easter festivals. Statistics of Christmas Communicants are not available for before 1956, but the number who received Communion between 1956 and 1968 declined by just over 10 per cent, from 57 per 1,000 population over the age of 15 to 51 per thousand. Easter Communicants can be considered over a longer period. In 1911, 98 per thousand population received Communion at Church of England altars on Easter Day. By 1922 this figure had fallen to 85 and, although it rose to 90 in 1925, the general pattern is one of steady decline to 63 in 1958. In 36 years the total decline was just under 26 per cent. Between 1958 and 1968 the graph shows a much sharper dip, from 63 to 51 Communicants per 1,000 – a decline of 20 per cent in ten years. In the 50-year period the overall decline was almost 50 per cent. Any interpretation of these figures must take account of the fact that Christmas and Easter Communicants provide a notoriously unreliable guide to the actual strength of a parish church. These are the occasions on which many people with a tenuous church connexion put in an appearance at the altar, never to be seen again during the rest of the year. Even so, declines of this magnitude are significant and cannot safely be ignored. They represent, in part, a fall in the number of regular churchgoers who once played an active part in the life of the church; they also form part of a picture of community withdrawal from the church which has already been noticed in the case of Baptisms and Confirmations.

The pioneers of synodical government who caused electoral rolls to be compiled in the early 1920s were hopeful that a vast army of lay members of the Church of England would rush to participate in the government of their church and that those who registered as electors would take their responsibilities seriously at the annual parochial meeting. There was no such rush, but a large number of people had their names entered on the rolls and in 1924 there were over 3½ million voters. This was more than the number of Easter Communicants at the time, though the annual meetings were never packed as the great majority of the electorate did not trouble to attend. Gradually the size of the rolls was reduced, though it was not until the end of World War II that the total fell below 3 millions. In 1954 it was 2,897,000, representing 94 in 1,000 of the eligible population of the country, but during those 30 years the population of England had grown considerably and the proportionate decline was nearly 33 per cent. By 1964 there was a further decline of 14 per cent, and another six per cent fall was indicated in 1968. A great deal of this is undoubtedly explicable in terms of pruning the rolls so that they could represent more realistically the active strength of the local churches. Pruning proved to be somewhat difficult since it was impossible to remove names from rolls without the express permission of the individuals concerned, and it was not until 1972 that the new Synodical Government Act required voters to re-register every six years.[6] Electoral roll statistics must, therefore, be treated with considerable caution but, in view of the general pattern of decline elsewhere, it is hardly surprising that they display a downward trend.

Much more precise – and infinitely more significant – are the statistics relating to ordinations. Although the Anglican priest is not isolated from the rest of the church in quite the same way as is his Roman Catholic brother, the Church of England has always been – and still is – a highly clericalized community. The vicar has a key role in the life of the local church. It may be argued that his role should change, but for the moment he is in a position to determine, for better or for worse, a great deal of the church's life. The number and quality of the clergy is quite crucial to the health of the Church of England as

[6] The new figures are not yet available.

it is at present organized. Hence the cause of widespread concern among those – the overwhelming majority – who hope that the present pattern of ministry will be maintained into an indefinite future.

The problem of securing an adequate supply of suitable men for the ordained ministry has dogged the Church of England for most of the 20th century. From an all-time peak of 23,670 in 1901, the number of clergymen had fallen to 18,196 by 1951. During this time the population of England had increased from 30.6 million to 41.3 million. Thus the ratio of clergymen to population had declined from 1 : 1,295 to 1 : 2,271. Soon after the end of the Second World War, it was estimated that upwards of 600 men would need to be ordained every year in order to offset losses by retirement and death. When only 505 (the highest figure for several years) were ordained in 1958, it was noted that the net loss of ordained manpower in that year was 127. As a proportion of the 18,000 clergymen at work in the provinces of Canterbury and York, this was of course quite small, yet it meant that a further 127 parishes were without a vicar or lacked an assistant curate. Little prescience was needed to realize that if annual losses continued at this rate for ten years the manpower of each of the 43 dioceses would be depleted by 30. Hence the sounding of alarm signals at Church House, Westminster and in many episcopal palaces. The effect was salutary. 605 men were ordained in 1961, while losses during that year were only 417. In 1963, 636 were ordained, more than offsetting 435 retirements and deaths. A considerable gap remained between the number of clergymen at work in the parishes and the number the Church of England believed itself to need, but the position was certainly improving. Leslie Paul, not normally given to euphoria and as cautious as befits a sociologist, felt able to comment in his report on what appeared to be an encouraging trend. After noting that the lines on the graph for recruitment and losses had crossed over, he added, 'The church may not therefore, as was once feared, face an actual shrinkage of men in the active ministry, but rather an increase.'[7] He went

[7] Leslie Paul, *op. cit.*, p. 22.

on to point out that the anticipated increase would not however keep pace with the projected rise in population.

In fact, the encouragement of the early 1960s was short-lived. By 1965 the number ordained had fallen to 592 and by 1969 it was down to 436. Another disturbing factor which began to emerge at this time was the increasing age of the clergy. In 1901, just over 45 per cent of them were under 44 years of age, but in 1963 only 31 per cent were under 44. In 1901, 17 per cent were over 65; in 1963 this figure had risen to over 25 per cent, and more than 2,300 were over 75. The latest published figures indicate that at the end of 1969 the number of priests under 44 comprised 40 per cent of the total, while only 9 per cent were over 65. This improvement in the situation was brought about by better pension arrangements and the increase in recruiting during the early part of the decade, but the same figures revealed that within the next ten years a total of 5,996 would reach retirement age, thus underlining the need for an annual intake of 600 men simply to keep pace with inevitable losses.

It was therefore hardly surprising that considerable alarm was expressed at a meeting of the General Synod held in February 1972, following the news that there had been only 392 ordinations during the previous year – the lowest figure for 12 years. Various explanations were offered: the Advisory Council for the Church's Ministry, which is responsible for the initial selection of candidates for training, had raised its standards; some members of the Synod said that young men were no longer prepared to commit themselves to the maintenance of large buildings which now housed only small congregations; the 'trivial' character of much of a priest's work was mentioned; a cathedral dean said that 100 clergymen were leaving the parochial ministry every year and were going into other full-time jobs such as teaching and social welfare; there was talk of the need to ordain more auxiliary priests who would continue in their secular occupations and minister in parishes at weekends. But the debate revealed neither the clarity of vision nor the common mind necessary for dealing creatively with a crisis situation.

It has seemed important to deal with the statistics of decline in some detail in order that consideration of the present position of the Church of England might be grounded in reality. Whenever the gravity of this position is discussed in public, it is not long before a dignitary or a parish priest – sometimes several of each – from a salubrious part of Surrey or Hertfordshire protests that the situation, far from deteriorating, is actually improving all the time. The churches in the area where he ministers are always comfortably full, their annual incomes are rising, every Saturday provides its ample quota of weddings and the church is beginning to show real concern for the needs of society. If only the wild men from Southwark and Cambridge would cease sounding false alarms and concentrate on solid pastoral work there would not be the slightest cause for concern – so the protest continues. But, even without the chilly blast of hard statistics, the majority of the parish clergy and an increasing number of the laity recognize that the Church of England, in common with every other church in the country, is now in a period when support for religious institutions is declining dramatically. Those who have spent more than 30 years in the ordained ministry are well aware that their work is, in almost every way, infinitely more difficult than it was when they first ministered in an English parish. The statistics simply confirm their subjective experiences, and many of them are exceedingly depressed.

This is understandable. The Christian faith is very precious to them. Few of them committed themselves to the ordained ministry because they had nothing better to do; the prime motivation was a deep and burning conviction about the Christian gospel. They believe that men and women would lead happier and more fulfilled lives if they could accept the claims of Christ and express their obedience to him through membership of the church. To such men, the sight of communities – large and small – in which only a tiny minority care about the church, and the things it stands for, is dispiriting. The position seems worse because, within living memory, the buildings in which they minister housed much larger congregations

and the church was at the centre of a considerable network of flourishing activity. That nearly-empty building
and the daily struggle to keep the Christian community
in existence seems to spell failure in large letters. Nor are
clergy in situations of this kind assisted by the utterances
of bishops and archdeacons who, drawing on the experience of almost half a century ago, assert that 'A
house-going parson makes a church-going people' or that
'The churches are always full where the priest says his
prayers and cares for his people.'

Yet, there is nothing in Christian theology and history
which suggests that the Christian faith ought to be
popular or that the church should attract vast numbers
of supporters. Jesus was evidently a much less successful
crowd-puller than 20th century evangelists like Dr. Billy
Graham and Dr. Oral Roberts. True, he once spoke to
5,000 people (a gathering which would be considered 'a
very poor evening' at a modern crusade in a huge sports
arena) but it seems that he was able to win the continuing support of only a handful of them and at the end of an
intensive and unique ministry his company of followers
was so small as to be almost inconsequential. The end
itself was hardly a triumph – at least, not in the way the
word is normally used. Death by crucifixion was the fate
of a criminal – one whom society found a nuisance and
wished to put out of the way. And the teaching which
Jesus gave to his followers included no promise of popularity or of spectacular success. On the contrary, he
warned them that they would meet hostility and in-
difference. The way of life to which they were called
was sure to be a hard one. Many of those who heard them
speaking would regard their message as offensive and
scandalous. This warning was necessary and timely, for
history suggests that every one of the apostles of Jesus
met death by martyrdom.

An examination of Christian history provides clear
evidence that the church was never intended to provide
a structure for a mass movement. It was to be – and still
is – the task of the church to share its Christian insights
and experiences with people in every part of the world.
The church was not designed to be an exclusive club,

neither was it told to court unpopularity. Yet the
Christian faith makes demands which not every man and
woman can meet. It calls for a level of sacrificial love
which no one can fully reach and which the overwhelming majority of mankind will never seek to attain. If the
church wishes to attract a large following it is obliged
to water-down the message entrusted to it by Jesus. There
have been many instances of its doing this, from the
conversion of Constantine onwards, and the final result
has always been corruption. A large and 'successful'
church must always be an object of great suspicion. A
church which occupies a dominating position in society
and exercises temporal power must inevitably be regarded
as ripe for reform. The church does not exist to win the
plaudits of the multitudes. Its role is that of a humble
servant, living under the sign of the cross.

Much confusion has arisen in the realm of theology
and, thus, in the life of the church through a false
equation of the concept of the Kingdom of God and the
institutional structures of the Christian community. The
Christian gospel is concerned with the Kingdom of God
– with the conviction that the world belongs to God and
that his purpose for the world is best realized when
human beings live together in freedom, justice and harmony. This was the essential teaching of Jesus and it
must always be the teaching of those who claim to be
his followers. The church enters into this world-view as
a community of people who are committed to the quest
for freedom, justice and harmony in society as a whole
and who are also committed to the expression of these
values within their own corporate life. The church is a
servant of the Kingdom and a sign of the Kingdom, but
it is not itself the Kingdom of God. It exists to offer the
world those insights into the nature of the Kingdom
which have been entrusted to it by Jesus and to present a
living illustration of the Kingdom in action.[8] It follows
from this that the church will always have a minority
role in relation to the Kingdom of God. The majority of
those who promote harmony, justice and freedom do so

[8] For a fuller discussion of this see *Do We Need the Church?* by
Richard P. McBrien, William Collins Sons & Co Ltd, 1969.

without committing themselves to membership of the church. They are citizens of the Kingdom – whether they recognize the fact or not – but they do not belong to the community of faith. So the church accepts for itself the images provided by Jesus in certain of his parables – yeast, salt and light.

Once these images are accepted and the church sees its true role in relation to the Kingdom of God anxieties about institutional size and success begin to fade away. The chief concern of the priest and the Christian congregation is not the enlargement of the church, but the enlargement of the Kingdom. Their own contributions to its enlargement are relatively small, but they are sensitive to those signs of the growth of the Kingdom in the community where they live and in the world at large. Here is their chief source of encouragement and hope. The fact that God is achieving more outside the church than within it is an occasion for rejoicing. The size of the church hardly matters if the Kingdom is advancing on many other human fronts.

Seen against this background of basic Christian belief, it may well be wondered why the current decline in the numerical strength of the Church of England has led to such a lowering of morale. Much of the work for individuals and local communities carried out by the church when it was larger in the latter part of the 19th century is now undertaken – usually with more adequate resources – by the state. The result has been an advance in the life of the Kingdom of God and the process has not been hindered by the decline of the church. Why, then, should ecclesiastical countenances be so grim?

Part of the explanation is to be found in the fact that many churchmen have not yet perceived the true relationship between the gospel, the Kingdom and the church. Of those who have, quite a number have yet to allow their perception to take full control of their normal thoughts and actions. But there is another problem which is the cause of most of the frustration and anxiety. When it is accepted by a clergyman and a local congregation that their vocation is to form a quite small community which will be a servant and a sign of the Kingdom of

God, they are liberated from bondage to many of those elements in the Christian tradition which, in present circumstances, are inhibiting to real life. Yet they are still obliged to function within – and to maintain – an ecclesiastical apparatus which was designed not to facilitate the life of a small group but to express the life of a large community. An obvious example of this is to be seen in those many parishes where there is a large mediaeval building. These were erected by and for the inhabitants of a sacral society in which church and community were so finely woven together as to be indistinguishable. The embattled tower symbolized the sovereignty of God over the surrounding neighbourhood; it also served as a place of refuge in time of war. The building was a meeting place for many functions besides worship, for the entire community; hence its size. The priest was involved closely in the lives of all who lived in the parish and was provided with – or exacted – the means of support to enable him to fulfil his accepted role.

Little imagination is needed – though it is sadly lacking in many influential quarters – to discern that it is virtually impossible for a small group of Christians, with an accepted minority role, to function effectively in such a setting. When the same group is also required to maintain the framework of this mediaeval setting in terms of buildings, organization and ministry, its life becomes a caricature of what the church is meant to be. Hence the intense frustration and depression now felt by many who are involved in the work of the Church of England's parish churches. They seem to be – and in fact are – fighting a losing battle to maintain their Christian integrity. Their time, energy and money are devoted to the maintenance of an inheritance which long since ceased to be useful and has now become a millstone round their necks. In certain parts of the country this millstone weighs less heavily. The pattern of local community life and the degree of community attachment to the church, especially in its architectural manifestations, still allows priests and congregations with zeal and imagination to function with a certain degree of effectiveness. These are the lucky ones and they continue to find fulfilment in their ministry to the neighbourhood. But, in the changed and changing climate of the 20th century, their numbers are rapidly decreasing and many of them are destined to join the ranks of those who feel imprisoned by an ecclesiastical system which will not allow them to express their Christian convictions in a credible form.

This is the crisis caused by numerical decline in the Church of England. The shrinkage of size hardly matters, and may lead to a tougher and more vigorous Christian community. But this can hardly be expected to happen while those who remain in the church are condemned to operate a machine which belongs to another age and can only be persuaded into movement by dint of massive effort leading to exhaustion. The reluctance of a new generation, which is not indifferent to the religious dimension, to restore the church's depleted ranks is closely related to this situation.

chapter 4

Parishes and Priests

The cumbersome machine which the Church of England is now required to operate was invented by and for a rural society. An extremely clever invention it was, too. Usually credited to Theodore of Tarsus, who was Archbishop of Canterbury from 668–690, the parochial system was designed so as to enable the church to function within every recognizable community. Some historians believe that the roots of this system may be traced to the pre-Christian era when landowners were required to make provision for the religious needs of their dependants, including the appointment of pagan priests to supervise the worship. Whatever its precise origins, the parochial system was developed for the small and simple communities of what the 20th century would regard as under-developed nations.

Britain hardly comes within that category now, yet the parochial system has not been significantly modified since the 13th and 14th centuries when the great majority of English parishes were given their present shape. The boundaries of a large number of parishes are still defined by lines drawn on maps compiled by mediaeval bishops and abbots. It occasions no surprise, therefore, to discover that the Church of England retains a heavy rural bias. 'Never forget that sooner or later you will become a country priest', was the parting advice given by a famous theological college principal to his students in the 1950s, and the same advice would be equally apposite twenty years later. Of the 11,162 parishes in existence on 31 December 1969, 6,252 had populations of less than 3,000 and 3,624 of them had populations of under 1,000. In a paper entitled 'A Critical Analysis of the Redeployment of the Clergy and a Possible Solution'

A. B. Miskin showed that in December 1958 there were 5,022 parishes with a population under 1,500.[1] The existence of so many small rural parishes is not of course a problem in itself. On the contrary these parishes are an indication of the church's continuing concern for every community, be it large or small, and they provide the means for ministering to every community. The problem, which has now reached crisis point, derives from the fact that the rural parishes attract a totally disproportionate amount of the Church of England's resources of money and clerical manpower. The clearest message to come from the 1964 Paul Report was that the clergy are located where the people are not.

A comparison between the dioceses of London and Oxford illustrates the point with some precision. Each diocese has approximately the same number of parishes (London 510, Oxford 508) but the population of London diocese is $3\frac{3}{4}$ millions, while that of Oxford is $1\frac{1}{2}$ millions. London has only 55 parishes with populations of under 3,000, whereas Oxford has 376 in this category. London has 372 parishes of more than 5,000 people (including 133 of more than 10,000) but Oxford has only 69 parishes with more than 5,000 people. At the end of 1969, London diocese had 764 clergymen on its books, Oxford had 562. Translated into terms of pastoral care, in London there is one clergyman for every 4,964 people, whereas in Oxford (which covers the counties of Oxford, Buckinghamshire and Berkshire) there is one clergyman for every 2,751 people. An even more vivid illustration of the problem is offered by a comparison of the south London diocese of Southwark and the rural diocese of Hereford. Only 13 of Hereford's 214 parishes have populations in excess of 3,000, but only 30 of Southwark's 308 parishes are below 3,000. In terms of pastoral responsibility, Hereford has one clergyman for every 1,293 people; Southwark has one for every 4,348 people. Birmingham has one for every 6,100 people.

If figures of this kind were produced for the medical and teaching professions, or for a commercial undertaking,

[1] *Prism*, December 1963.

immediate action would be called for – and taken. Do they matter when the institution is the church? If church attendances are to be taken as a guide – the Church of England still regards sharing in worship as significant – the answer is certainly Yes. Easter Communicants in London diocese in 1968 averaged 28 per 1,000 of the population; in Oxford they were 68 per 1,000. Hereford averaged 134 per 1,000, Southwark only 35. Birmingham was lowest with 27. Attendances on ordinary Sundays reflect a similar pattern. Whether or not people attend church is of course controlled by many influences unrelated to the presence of clergymen in the locality. Throughout Europe, church attendances in urban areas are lower than in rural areas. But A. B. Miskin's research indicates that the presence of full-time workers in a parish does make some difference to the number of people who share in worship. After analysing the statistics of parishes of varying size and locality, Miskin concluded, 'Increasing population adds ten more Christmas communicants per extra 1,000, whereas one extra full-time worker adds eighty to ninety, irrespective of population, though with diminishing effect per additional worker.'[2] No statistics are required to demonstrate that if a priest is serving a smaller population the people are likely to get better pastoral care and that if a priest is struggling, single-handed, with a vast urban parish the church is unlikely to be given vigorous leadership.

There are additional causes for anxiety. One of these concerns the work load of rural clergy. When the population of a parish falls below 1,000 it is not easy for a man to find full-time employment within the life of the local church or in the community at large. There were 3,624 such parishes (almost one-third of the total) at the end of 1969. Some of them have elderly vicars, for whom they offer a gentle transition to retirement, but a large number are served by young or middle-aged men who either find outlets for their surplus energy in extra-parochial activity or are driven to deep frustration. When they offered themselves for ordination most of them had

[2] *ibid.*

a vision of full-time service of Christ in the church, and they were led to believe by the church that this would be their lot. The maintenance of an 8-bedroom vicarage with a 2-acre garden is hardly an adequate substitute for 'the care of souls'. When there is added the experience of Sunday services attended by a mere handful of people and the problem of keeping a large mediaeval building in good repair, it is not difficult to understand why the morale of the country clergy is now so low.

If the Church of England were replete with manpower and money, it would still be necessary to deal with this important human problem. In fact, it is desperately short of both. There is hardly an urban area in England that is adequately staffed with clergy and even if the priests were available these areas could not find the money for their stipends. Yet men are languishing in country parishes and each one is being subsidized by £800–1,000 a year from central church funds, since the ancient endowments rarely yield more than £500 a year. The Morley Commission, which published its Report in 1967, offered a devastatingly frank judgement on the situation: 'The present way in which the church handles the care, deployment and the payment of the clergy is inadequate and wasteful. It fails to meet contemporary needs. It distorts the image of the church as a divinely constituted society. Consequently it ought to be replaced by another.'[3]

Five years later the system is still waiting to be replaced and the failure of the Church of England to accept and implement the findings and recommendations of the Morley Commission is a symptom of the same disorder that led to the rejection of the Anglican-Methodist unity scheme. Three obstacles stand in the way of a rational deployment of the clergy. The first consists of stipends and housing. The endowments which provide the basic stipend for a priest are attached to particular places and neither the endowment nor the income from it can be diverted elsewhere, except in very special circumstances. Parsonage houses obviously stand in their parishes and,

---

[3] *Partners in Ministry*, p. 5, Church Information Office, 1967.

though sites can be sold, the proceeds of a sale must normally remain in the parish concerned. The result is that clergy must be deployed, not where they are most needed but where stipends and housing are available to provide for their material needs. Since the endowment of most parishes now requires a substantial supplement from central church funds, the financial aspect of deployment is less significant than was once the case, but it is still a factor to be reckoned with and the problems associated with the housing of clergy, particularly in areas of dense population, are often insuperable.

The second obstacle is much more formidable and involves the methods by which clergy are given their appointments. Those who are not closely acquainted with the Church of England are usually astonished to be told that bishops are responsible for only 30 per cent of the appointments to parishes in their dioceses. The Crown controls seven per cent through the nominations of the Queen, the Lord Chancellor, the Duchies of Cornwall and Lancaster and the Home Secretary. A further seven per cent are in the hands of universities, colleges and schools, and six per cent of all parochial appointments are made by the Deans and Chapters of cathedrals. Ten per cent are made by the clergy of ancient parishes from whose territory new parishes have been created and two per cent by Diocesan Boards of Patronage. That appointments to parishes are made by bodies such as these may well appear strange, but some fairly reasonable explanation can normally be offered. Far less easy to explain and justify is the fact that 16 per cent of clergy appointments are made by religious patronage trusts and societies, and 22 per cent by private individuals. The religious patronage trusts, the majority of which were formed in the 19th century, are avowedly partisan and propagandist in their aims and in their choice of nominees. They exist to promote either an Anglo-catholic or an evangelical viewpoint and no priest who has not been declared 'sound' in theological wind and limb can expect to receive an appointment at their hands. They are responsible for appointments to about 1,800 parishes. Private patronage owes its origin to the past when the Lord of the Manor or some other landowner had the right to appoint the local parish priest. These rights have changed hands with the passage of time (until the present century they were saleable assets; hence the acquisition of patronage by the party trusts) and nominations are now made by a great variety of individuals and corporate bodies. Dukes, earls, marchionesses, baronets, admirals, colonels, city livery companies, collieries, executors and many other improbable patrons are permitted to nominate about 2,500 priests to leadership of local churches. Leaving on one side the propriety or otherwise of nominations from these quarters, it is obvious that the existence of these many points of nomination makes anything approaching a comprehensive and calculated appointments system quite impossible. The situation which now exists as a result was described cogently and with unrivalled authority by the Archbishop of Canterbury in a speech to the Church Assembly on 6 July 1967. Dr. Ramsey was speaking of the position of a typical young priest who is ready for appointment as vicar of a parish and discusses the possibilities with his bishop: 'The bishop says to him, "I think you had better go there." But if the bishop were honestly obliged to think aloud and to expose all his thoughts, as on the Day of Judgement, the bishop would be heard saying something like this: "Of course, this young man is just the man I should like to see in this very important town sphere, but it has a body of patrons; they wouldn't appoint him, and it is not my appointment. That's out." Or: "This is a man who perhaps some other bishop might use very well in this place or that place. But I know the Bishop of X is trying to find jobs for a long list of his own curates, so we won't try that." Then, most tragic of all, there is the large parish which has had an incumbent for years and years and years and is being very badly looked after and really does need a change for the sake of the souls of the people, and one would love to put forward this particular, ardent young priest, but it is impossible to do so because of the operation of the freehold.'

The Archbishop might also have mentioned that there is no comprehensive source of information which enables

anyone responsible for making an appointment to know
who is available and what their particular qualifications,
experience and interests may be. *Crockford's Clerical
Directory*, edited and produced by Oxford University
Press, provides a complete list of the clergy but the bio-
graphical material is, of necessity, somewhat sketchy. It
is possible to discover from *Crockford's* a man's full name,
his educational background and academic attainments,
together with the posts he has held since ordination. This
is better than nothing, but it is hardly sufficient evidence
upon which to approach a priest about a particular post.
How, then, does a bishop or patron find his man? A conversation with a fellow bishop over dinner at the Athenaeum, or a letter to another bishop, may lead to the un-
earthing of a suitable priest for a vacant parish, though
it is unlikely that a bishop will want to part with his
most able men unless the post is one of very special
responsibility. The Crown has its own files, which are
said to be full of interesting information about clergymen,
but no one is quite clear how a priest qualifies for admission to this company; a chaplaincy in one of the armed
services is not unhelpful. The trusts obviously have their
own carefully vetted lists of clergymen holding eccentric
theological views. But the main source of information
for bishops and private patrons is the old boy network.
The Revd. John X is appointed to 'the cure of souls' in
this or that parish because the friend of a friend of a
cathedral canon met the bishop's chaplain at a cocktail
party. A chance remark in the cloakroom after a church
meeting can make all the difference to the sphere of a
priest's future ministry and to the life of a particular
parish. No one need doubt that the Lord of the church is
well able to work through cocktail parties and cloak-
rooms, but if the universe as a whole is reliable evidence
concerning his methods it might well be concluded that
he would normally operate through more orderly
channels. The church's old boy network is not a sinister
device – in the absence of any rational appointments
system there is no other way of working – but it is
highly inefficient. Since human beings are not omniscient,
it is impossible for any one person to know everyone – or

even all the 18,205 clergymen who might be considered
for a vacant parish. Even a diocesan staff meeting attended
by, say, two bishops, two archdeacons, a dean, four
canons and several officials can only know a limited
number of priests. When a particular appointment is
under consideration at such a meeting, the field of choice
is normally quite small and, all too often, a less than
ideal decision is made simply because no other priest
is known to be available. Private patrons obviously are
even less well informed. On the other hand, a very large
number of priests would welcome the chance to move
from their present parishes to a new sphere of work, but
they are not aware that certain places are vacant nor
is the person responsible for the appointment aware of
their existence, much less of their gifts and needs. Jobs
are but rarely advertised, except in the case of assistant
curacies, and 'it is not done' to apply for an unadvertised
post; to ask to be considered for any work in the Church
of England is normally the surest way of being dis-
qualified from consideration, though bishops are normally
quite happy to place the name of a priest on a waiting list
provided the man's present bishop is agreeable. The
suggestion of the Paul and Morley Reports that the
Church of England should have an open appointments
system, involving the advertising of all vacant posts, was
given a hostile reception and denounced from various
quarters, sometimes on the grounds that it would encourage corruption, sometimes out of fear that it might
introduce commercial efficiency into the church. Both
objections seemed to derive from a somewhat cynical
view of an institution which makes high claims about
its insights and the nature of its corporate life.

The freehold, which gives a rector or vicar 'a freehold
interest in the emoluments of the benefice until his death
or until the benefice is otherwise legally vacated by
him',[4] is the third major obstacle to the proper deployment of the clergy. Until 1947 an incumbent could only
be removed from his parish if he had been convicted of
certain serious offences by the courts or been found guilty

[4] *Halsbury's Laws of England*, volume 13 section 438, 3rd edition,
Butterworth & Co, 1957.

of sexual immorality. Although the priest might be scandalously neglectful of his pastoral duties, nothing could take away his legal right to remain in the parish and draw the stipend. An attempt was made to deal with this unsatisfactory position by means of the Incumbents (Discipline) Measures, 1947 to 1953, which now allows proceedings to be taken in church courts against a priest 'for neglect of his duties or conduct unbecoming the character of a clerk in holy orders', but this has not proved to be very effective. The last case to be heard under these measures led to a protracted and unedifying trial in 1970, as a result of which the vicar of a parish in the West of England was found not guilty and the Church Commissioners had to find £30,000 to pay the bill for the legal costs. It will be a long time before any other 'aggrieved archdeacon' enters this expensive territory. The real problem of the freehold, however, is not the extreme case of neglect, but the more common situation in which a priest has contributed as much as he is able to a particular parish, or is misplaced, yet is unwilling to move elsewhere. Such a situation can be extremely painful for all concerned and obviously limits the power of a bishop to provide the parishes of his diocese with the best available leadership and to give his clergy the most appropriate spheres of work. The great majority of Church of England clergy – particularly the older men – are strenuously opposed to any modification in the freehold. Some aver that it safeguards their freedom to preach controversial truths and to take unpopular action, though an observer of the Anglican scene would be hard pressed to find any clergyman who is actually exploiting this freedom at the present time and the true prophet is normally the last man to look for legal protection. Others believe that the freehold protects them against the inconvenience of, as they say, 'being moved around like pawns on a chessboard', and they often cite examples of Roman Catholic priests who are alleged to have received letters from their bishops on Monday morning ordering them to be in some other parish by the next Friday lunchtime. The common factor in both instances is mistrust of the bishops by the parochial clergy; the freehold is seen as offering protection against the machinations of unscrupulous, ruthless, insensitive or merely incompetent men in episcopal orders. This is not the moment to discuss the virtues and vices of the Church of England's bishops, which in any case vary considerably, as one might expect, but it may be noted in passing that some Free Churchmen are beginning to wonder why episcopacy is paraded before them as essential to Christian ministry, and to any church unity scheme, when parish priests insist on retaining legal safeguards against the possible actions of their bishops.

During the 1960s two attempts were made to overcome the most pressing problems arising from the Church of England's inability to deploy its resources where, in a rapidly changing society, they are most needed. The first of these was a relatively modest set of proposals, which nonetheless occupied the Church Assembly in discussions lasting over a period of two years and led to the promulgation in 1969 of a 101-page legal document known as *The Pastoral Measure*. This brought together a number of earlier pieces of legislation dealing with buildings, appointments, boundaries, etc. and made provision for certain new steps to be taken in situations where the church is finding it difficult, if not actually impossible, to discharge its pastoral responsibilities. Every diocese now has a pastoral committee, consisting of members of the diocesan hierarchy and representatives of the clergy and laity. This committee advises the bishop on the pastoral needs of the diocese, particularly in those parts of it where reorganization is called for. A church building may be declared redundant and its parish merged with another to form a larger pastoral unit. If the vicar of the redundant church is uncooperative, he can be removed, but he must be offered an equivalent appointment elsewhere or agreed compensation for loss of office. This provision now makes possible a considerable degree of reorganization in towns where buildings erected during the Victorian era of expansion are clearly redundant and the present parish boundaries are unrelated to new patterns of community. Some dioceses have begun to make use of this new freedom, and more will doubtless

do so as *The Pastoral Measure* is more widely understood
and accepted, but it is extremely difficult to move when
there is local resistance, and a log jam in appointments
to vicarages, which has been a problem since 1967, has
not made it easy for the clergy of redundant parishes to
be offered other appointments. Another new departure
is the right of the bishop, acting with the consent of his
Pastoral Committee, to suspend further appointments to
parishes which have become vacant. This is proving to
be useful in country areas where small parishes are now
being amalgamated. It is also useful in towns where major
reorganization schemes are being planned. In both situations patrons are prevented from hindering pastoral advance by making appointments to parishes which either
do not need the full-time services of a priest or need to be
considered in relation to the requirements of a wider area.
Provision is also made for the transfer of endowments
from one parish to another, or to the diocesan stipends
fund. Recent years have seen a number of experiments
in group and team ministries, enabling several clergymen
to function together over an area which previously might
have encompassed several independent parishes. Because
of their experimental character, groups and teams have
been very vulnerable to changes in personnel and policy
at diocesan and local levels, but *The Pastoral Measure*
provides a legal framework to give them an appropriate
degree of security and stability. A priest may now have
the status and responsibilities of a vicar without having
to conform to the established legal requirements for such
posts. Parishes can be created or kept in being even
though they have no consecrated building for worship
– another facility which makes possible certain experimental forms of ministry. These are modest provisions
and do nothing to tackle the fundamental problems
which underlie the Church of England's inability to re-
deploy its considerable pastoral resources. Nonetheless,
they offer certain opportunities which have yet to be fully
exploited and a degree of freedom which, though hardly
to be thought of in terms of liberation, is greater than anything previously experienced by the Established Church.

Infinitely more radical in its approach and dramatic

in its proposals was the Commission appointed by the Church Assembly in 1965 to consider the deployment and payment of the clergy in the light of the Paul Report (1964) and certain smaller reports and debates on the same subject. Meeting under the chairmanship of Canon W. Fenton Morley (then Vicar of Leeds, now Dean of Salisbury), the Commission, which was made up of a very able – and mainly progressive – group of bishops, priests and laity, produced its report in the summer of 1967[5] and caused a considerable stir in the Church of England. It was proposed that the parson's freehold and the existing patronage system should be abolished. Every clergyman would be on the books of a particular diocese and be guaranteed financial support whether or not he was in employment. Appointments to parishes would be made by a Diocesan Ministry Commission, consisting of the bishop and archdeacons of the diocese, together with representatives of the clergy and laity. A Central Ministry Commission was suggested as the coordinating body for the country as a whole, facilitating the movement of clergy from one diocese to another. Appointments would be for a term of years, with the possibility of renewal by mutual consent, or without term of years but subject to review. Retirement at a specified age would be compulsory and a bishop or priest could only remain in office by consent of the appointing body. A Central Payment Authority would be responsible for the stipends of all the clergy on a scale to be determined by the Church Assembly or its successor, the General Synod. The Diocesan Ministry Commission and the Diocesan Pastoral Committee would cooperate closely in matters relating to pastoral reorganization, enabling the church to create viable and adequately-staffed parish units. The Report made provision for existing holders of offices to retain them on the present terms if they so desired, and it was also suggested that an appeals machinery be established for the benefit of anyone who believed that the new system was working unfairly against the interests of individuals or of the church in a particular area.

[5] *Partners in Ministry*, Church Information Office, 1967.

In presenting these proposals, the Morley Commission expressed its belief that if translated into positive action they 'would enable the Church of England to use its resources to far better advantage; and, generally, to engage its ministry at the points of greatest need, at moments when these needs manifest themselves and not after they have given way to others.'[6] But the Commission was emphatic that its proposals must be treated as a unity. Each was part of an interlocking and finely balanced scheme which had been designed to serve the contemporary needs of an ancient institution and the many different people who had been ordained to its full-time service. Remove one or more of the elements in the scheme and the whole thing would be destroyed. Select just a few items for implementation and the Church of England's chief problem would remain. So the Commission argued – with cogency – and they had the support of the Archbishop of Canterbury who said that, although he had initially been hesitant about certain of the proposals, he had come to see that the whole scheme hung together and reflected a new spirit and a new approach to the future of the church. He warned, however, that if the proposals were to be carried a very great body of conviction and enthusiasm would be needed in the church.

In the event, this conviction and enthusiasm was not forthcoming. Many clergy were fearful about the possible consequences of the loss of their freehold. The patronage trusts and societies immediately sprang to the defence of their 'property'. The idea of appointments being made by a diocesan commission was generally unpopular, few people realizing that a considerable number of appointments are already made by committees – the bishop's staff meeting, a college livings committee, a trust committee. Bogies of many shapes and sizes were produced for inspection, but the most determined and formidable opposition came from men like the Bishop of Chester (Dr. Gerald Ellison) who perceived, correctly, that implementation of the Morley proposals would gradually change the whole structure of the Church of England and

6 *ibid*, p. 1.

remove quite a number of those things which, for reasons good and bad, they valued in the traditional system – or lack of it. The Report constituted a programme for major reform and was, therefore, highly suspect.

There are three main ways in which reforms can be blocked. One is to reject the proposals out of hand. Another is to amend the proposals so drastically that they bear little, if any, resemblance to their original form. The third is to produce a new set of proposals which, while acknowledging the need for change and the important contribution made by those who have gone before, destroy the original work and buttress the *status quo*. The Church Assembly, accepting the expert guidance of the Bishop of Chester, chose the third way when called upon, towards the end of its life, to make a decision about the Morley Report. In July 1970 the Assembly asked for a Terms of Ministry Committee, which was charged to prepare, in consultation with the Church Commissioners and the Pensions Board, and in the light of the Report *Partners in Ministry* and the subsequent discussion of that Report, a scheme which would deal with a number of matters – in particular, the reform of the patronage system, the dissolution under certain circumstances of the pastoral relationship between a vicar and his parish, the age of retirement for clergy, arrangements for the effective employment of available manpower, and a more equitable structure for remuneration of clergy. The Committee came into existence in the Spring of 1971, with the Bishop of Manchester in its chair and a weak membership. Predictably, the first Report published in June 1972 bore little relationship to the Morley proposals. At the outset it stressed that it was not a 'package' deal; any of the proposals could be accepted or rejected independently, since they did not constitute an inter-related and substantial programme of reform. A Central Stipends Authority was proposed and it was suggested that this might consult with and advise the dioceses in matters related to the payment of the clergy. The pooling of endowments and glebe revenues was recommended, but the process to take place only when the present beneficiaries moved elsewhere. The House of Bishops was invited to

C

appoint a working group to determine how the available clerical manpower might be fairly shared and to produce guidelines. The committee saw no need for a central register of the clergy to be compiled, but thought that the Archbishops of Canterbury and York should have an Adviser on Appointments who would maintain a list of clergy who wished to move and generally facilitate the movement of 15,000 priests to appropriate spheres of work. A division of opinion was registered over the exercising of patronage. Some members of the committee were ready to settle for closer consultation between those with an interest in a particular appointment. Others (the majority) favoured the setting up of Parish Appointment Committees, made up of bishop, patron and parish representatives, which would select priests for particular parishes. A compulsory retirement age of 70 was proposed for the elderly and a diocesan committee or provincial tribunal for the delinquent. The Church Information Office described these changes as 'sweeping'. They were warmly welcomed by the General Synod a month later, though the suggestion about Parish Appointment Committees was referred back with a request that it should be considered in the light of an overall deployment policy. This could be significant but the strength of the opposition to the reference back suggests that nothing very dramatic will receive final approval.

It is clear, then, that no fundamental change in the Church of England's method of deploying its ordained manpower is likely within the foreseeable future. Many, though by no means all, of the most glaring abuses and absurdities will be eliminated or modified but the general structure will remain unchanged. In the light of the challenge which a changed and changing society is presenting to the church the consequences are, in the long term, likely to be extremely serious. Much good work will continue in the parishes, but inevitably it will be reduced in scope and quality as the resources of the church become more distant from the areas of greatest need. The facts about the present situation have been well documented and those who believe that statistics are never truthful have only to pay attention to what is happening in a cross-section of ordinary parishes. Yet there is a marked – and in some ways growing – disinclination to face the facts. Many of them are of course uncomfortable and threatening. They demand change and upheaval. They hint that some familiar landmarks may have to go. Like the proposals for Anglican-Methodist unity proposals, they threaten to undermine the security of many churchmen who, in a world of bewildering change, often cling to the institutional structures of the church with the desperation of those standing under sentence of death. The Church of England's crisis has a deep psychological content and this, rather than theological inadequacy, posits the greatest threat to the recovery of its well-being.

chapter 5

Liturgy and Chaos

A description of the condition of the Church of England in the early 1970s must of necessity give the general impression of a body of Christian people who are divided over many thing but are for the most part united in their resistance to change. In the sphere of worship, however, there has, over the past half century and more especially over the past 25 years, been unprecedented change. Viewed from one angle it may seem rather odd that change should have proved possible in this area, whereas a stubborn conservatism has asserted itself elsewhere. After all, forms of worship affect the Christian every time he sets foot in a church building for a public service. There is no missing changes here, but it would be possible to turn the whole of the church's administrative machinery upside down without the ordinary church member being greatly inconvenienced – or indeed conscious of the fact. On the other hand, the forms of worship which the Church of England inherited from the 16th and 17th centuries had become so manifestly unsatisfactory for the present age, that a growing number of those who were in weekly contact with them came to recognize the need for some degree of change. The 'Dearly beloved brethren' of the Methodist Church can be asked to wait for reunion; the 'Dearly beloved brethren' of the Book of Common Prayer must be dealt with as quickly as possible.

The greatest changes in Anglican worship have, however, been concentrated on the basic content, the form of presentation and the time of worship, rather than on the words which constitute the Prayer Book services. During the years immediately prior to 1939 the common pattern of Sunday worship in a parish church was:

8 a.m.   Holy Communion – without music.
11 a.m.   Morning Prayer or Solemn Eucharist –
           with music and sermon.
6.30 p.m. Evening Prayer – with music and sermon.

The attendance at 8 a.m. would never be large, except at major festivals. The atmosphere was quiet and devotional; individuals slipped in and out of church without establishing much contact with others in the congregation. At 11 a.m. bell-ringers and choir were on parade and in middle-class suburbia and country towns the congregation might be fairly large. In those places – the majority – where Morning Prayer provided the staple diet there was a marked degree of formality about the worship. The churchwardens and sidesmen carried the collection to the altar with a military bearing appropriate to survivors of the 1914–18 war; the social composition of congregations still reflected a little of the pre-1914 era when the better-off people attended church in the morning and their servants, together with other indigent members of society, in the evening. Where there was a Solemn Eucharist at 11 o'clock this was a sign of the influence of the 19th century Oxford Movement which had sought, with remarkable success, to restore the Church of England's heritage of Catholic theology and worship. In such parishes the congregation was more mixed, socially, and the ceremonial, though highly elaborate, was not too formal, reflecting the ethos of the Latin Church from which it was in fact mainly derived. The number of Communicants was normally quite small, being confined to the priest, the servers and a handful of people who were too old to attend the eight o'clock service for Communion but not too frail to fast until mid-morning. Evening services in churches of both traditions tended to be rather more folksy, but were bound by the form of Evening Prayer, with its appointed psalms, Bible readings and prayers, and the inevitable sermon. In the more advanced Anglo-catholic churches the evening service sometimes took the form of Compline and Benediction, again borrowed from Latin quarters.

This pattern of Sunday worship may still be found in

certain places – particularly in large towns – but it has
largely disappeared from those areas where the church
is working among a residential population. The 8 a.m.
Holy Communion remains, largely in its old form, but
11 a.m. Morning Prayer has disappeared. Instead there
is the Parish Communion somewhere between the hours
of 9 and 10. This is often attended by fairly large congregations made up of people of all ages. Babies in prams
may be present, teenagers will be there (sometimes
accompanying the service with guitars and drums), and
a visitor would be especially conscious of family groups
sitting together. The service is less formal than Morning or Evening Prayer and the ceremonial, in contrast
with the old Solemn Eucharist, is simple, being designed
to emphasize the main features of the eucharistic action.
The bread and wine is carried to the Holy Table in an
offertory procession. The clergy often face the congregation for the whole of the service, and in those churches
where there is a long chancel an altar has been set up
in the nave to ensure a close relationship between the
action and the congregation. Invariably there are large
numbers of weekly communicants. The Ministry of the
Word is seen as an essential part of the worship and this
is emphasized by a Gospel procession and a sermon
based on the Bible readings for the day. These readings
may well be given by laypeople. Members of the congregation, in addition to joining vocally in most of the
prayers, also play a prominent part in leading certain
parts of the service. In some places laymen assist the
priest in the distribution of Communion, and the corporate nature of the action is frequently carried over
into a parish breakfast, or at least cups of coffee, served
after the service. Where the Parish Communion has
become the main act of worship on Sunday, it is usual
to find that the number of people attending Evening
Prayer is considerably reduced. This is due partly to the
general decline in churchgoing in recent decades, and
also to the fact that members of the Church of England
who intend to go to church once on Sunday now choose
the Parish Communion. In certain areas Evening Prayer
has followed Morning Prayer into desuetude but generally

it remains, even though sparsely attended. So completely does the Parish Communion dominate the Anglican scene that when new church buildings are required these are invariably designed to facilitate this form of worship, in which participation plays such an important part, and to embody the particular insights represented by what is commonly known as the Liturgical Movement. Circular, octagonal, elliptical, triangular buildings are the order of the day and, though post-war church building in England has been disastrously lacking in insight and inspiration, a handful of new buildings are functionally useful and aesthetically pleasing. It is not too much to say that the past twenty-five years have seen greater changes in the worship and architecture of the Church of England than anything experienced during the previous 400 years.

A key event was the publication in 1937 of a volume of essays entitled *The Parish Communion*. Edited by Father Gabriel Hebert, a monk of the Society of the Sacred Mission, the essays included theological and historical appraisals of the place of the Holy Communion in the life of the church down the ages, together with suggestions as to how the Holy Communion might be restored to 'its rightful place' in the Church of England. The scholarly and pastoral reputations of the contributors did not allow the volume to be ignored, and the writers were able to draw on the experience of certain isolated parishes in which there had been something closely akin to a Parish Communion for 20 years or more. Few, if any, collections of essays have had such a dramatic effect on the life of a church.

Their impact can, however, only be properly understood when two other factors are taken into account. Since the latter years of the 19th century there had been growing dissatisfaction with the forms of worship provided by the 1662 Prayer Book and disquiet at the extent to which those who felt moved to substitute other forms could flagrantly break the law of the land by disregarding the Act of Uniformity. There had been prosecutions of clergymen during Queen Victoria's time and some had even been committed to prison for conducting 'illegal

worship'. A Royal Commission was appointed to investi-
gate the situation and reported in 1906 that 'the law of
public worship in the Church of England is too narrow
for the religious life of the present generation.' It added:
'The machinery for discipline has broken down.' In
retrospect, it can be seen that this marked the end of a
long period in which the power of the state was employed
to impose uniformity of worship throughout the Church
of England, though a further 60 years were to pass before
the church was in a position to experiment with new
forms of service without first securing the agreement of
Parliament to its proposals. Soon after the Royal Commission had reported in 1906, the Convocations of Canterbury and York were sent Royal Letters of Business
authorizing them to report to the Crown on 'the desir-
ability and the form and contents . . . of any modifications
of the existing law relating to the conduct of Divine
Service and to the ornaments and fittings of churches.'
The Convocations, operating on the principle that change
should be kept to a minimum and should not involve anything suggesting changes of doctrine, had almost completed their work when the war broke out in 1914 and
prevented further progress. When the opportunity to continue came in 1918 they approached the task from a somewhat different angle. Instead of seeking minimum changes
to keep Parliament happy, the bishops began to consider
what would be the most appropriate liturgical forms for
the church to use in the new post-war era. This turned out
to be an arduous task since there was among the bishops,
as in the Church of England as a whole, a great diversity
of eucharistic doctrine. Furthermore, their proposals now
had to run the gauntlet of the newly-constituted Church
Assembly which, after many ill-informed and ill-tempered
debates, finally approved a revised Prayer Book in 1927.
This was submitted to Parliament but the activities of the
Church Assembly had caused the matter to become one of
public controversy, with the church's evangelical and
Anglo-catholic wings united in opposition. Parliament
rejected the new prayer book in 1927 and also an amended
version of it submitted a year later. So, as far as the law
was concerned, the Church of England was back to 1662,

but the bishops, showing an uncharacteristic disrespect for law and order, announced that 'during the present emergency and until further order be taken' they could not 'regard as inconsistent with loyalty to the principles of the Church of England the use of such additions or deviations as fall within the limits' of the 1928 Prayer Book.

In the event, the provisions of the new book were not very widely used because the Church of England as a whole did not care for them. But various elements from this source found their way into Anglican services, those who looked for inspiration to Rome rather than Canterbury continued along their well-established track and the Act of Uniformity had, deservedly, become an object of ridicule. The situation was summed up by a distinguished liturgist when he wrote in 1945: 'We have to face the facts that though the Church of England has an official liturgy more rigidly and minutely prescribed in its details than that of almost any other church in Christendom; and though its observance is fortified by a most complicated and formidable system of courts and legal penalties, such as no other religious society in history has ever found necessary to secure the observance of its rites, yet the Church of England today presents a liturgical disorganization such as is found in no other Christian body, and exhibits a liturgical diversity not commonly found in bodies which do not profess to have any set liturgy at all.'[1]

Father Hebert and his fellow-essayists were, therefore, addressing a church which was already beginning to emerge from the liturgical ice-age in which it had been held for several centuries. They were also reflecting, and were in fact deeply influenced by, a new liturgical movement which had been gathering momentum throughout Western Europe since the turn of the century. In 1903 Pope Pius X had issued directions designed to involve the Roman Catholic laity more closely in the offering of the Mass and during the whole of his reign, which lasted until 1914, he encouraged more frequent Communion. Within the great Benedictine abbeys of Maria

[1] *The Shape of the Liturgy* by Gregory Dix, p. 700, Dacre Press, 1945.

Laach and Maredsous scholars were delving deeply into
the origins and development of the Eucharistic rites and
gaining theological insights which, if taken seriously, were
bound to have a profound effect upon the forms of worship used by the contemporary church. From 1910 onwards
their work began to influence the way in which the Mass
was celebrated in many religious houses, and in some
parishes, in Germany, Belgium, Holland, France and
Spain. The number of these pioneering centres must not
be exaggerated, but they proved to be highly influential
and, although frequently denounced by cardinals and
bishops, prepared the way for the extensive reforms
promulgated in the Vatican II Constitution on the Sacred
Liturgy.

The fact that the Liturgical Movement, as it came to
be called, spread to England from Europe through the
Church of England, rather than through the Roman
Catholic Church in this country, provides an interesting
footnote to early 20th-century church history. The explanation is not difficult to find. English Catholicism, or
rather Irish Catholicism transferred to English soil, was
still insular and mainly preoccupied with establishing its
position in what had until quite recently been hostile
territory. Its leaders had little interest in liturgical matters
and felt little affinity with their brethren in Europe who
breathed the relaxed atmosphere of a majority position
in society. The Church of England was hardly less insular
in its outlook but Father Hebert, Dom Gregory Dix and
other monks established close relations with the monastic
centres of liturgical renewal in Europe, and the seeds they
brought home with them found receptive patches of soil
in Anglican territory. Although the Book of Common
Prayer was now seen as archaic and inadequate, it was
the intention of its 16th- and 17th-century compilers that
it should provide forms of worship for the English
church in which the entire congregation could share.
Although the services had come to be dominated by the
educated minister, who had slipped conveniently into the
position previously occupied by the sacerdotal priest,
many of the aims of the Liturgical Movement, and a little
of its theology, was implicit in the Church of England's

approach to worship which required services to be scriptural in content, intelligible in language and conduct, corporate in expression and related to the ordered worship of the whole church.

Naturally, the Second World War prevented much organized development from the 1937 essays, though there was a notable incident in 1942 when, at a crucial stage in the conflict, a proctor in the Convocation of Canterbury proposed that an approach should be made to Parliament about the position of the prayer of oblation in the Holy Communion service. The war years served, however, to make the need for liturgical change seem even more obvious and to create an atmosphere in which change might be more acceptable. In 1949 a group of parish priests and liturgists (including Father Hebert) met at The Queen's College, Birmingham to take stock of the post-war situation and, as a result, launched the Parish and People movement which was to be specially concerned with the renewal of worship in the parish churches and with assisting congregations to discover how the liturgical action in church could be carried forward into social action in the community. During the next decade local and national conferences were held, and upwards of 1,500 people (mainly clergy) recruited into membership. The growing popularity of the Parish Communion as an important act of Sunday worship caused some disquiet among the pioneers of the Liturgical Movement, for it seemed that many parishes were adopting the Parish Communion as 'a nice service', rather than as the expression of deep insights into the nature of the church. These insights were believed to demand that the Parish Communion should not be just one among a mixed programme of services from which parishioners could take their choice; on the contrary, it should be the focal point of the life of the local church – 'The Lord's People at the Lord's Service on the Lord's Day.' A good deal of the energies of Parish and People were, in consequence, devoted to advocating the need for careful teaching about the church and the liturgy both before and after the introduction of the Parish Communion in a parish. A survey carried out in 1961 indicated that some form of preparation had taken place in about one-third of the parishes[2] but it cannot be assumed from this that there is no proper understanding of the significance of the change in the rest. Commenting critically, yet with a certain sympathy, on the growth of the Parish Communion in the Church of England, Dr. Michael Ramsey said in 1955, 'In the long run it will be its own interpreter and teacher.'[3] This prophecy has come true. In the great majority of the parishes where the Parish Communion has become the chief act of worship there is an understanding of Christian commitment and responsibility, and a sense of purpose and liveliness, that were not there before.

Significantly, this very considerable change in the pattern of Anglican worship was able to develop without the aid of Prayer Book revision. The pioneers of the Liturgical Movement were certainly aware of the deficiencies of the 1662 Communion rite and they looked forward to the time when a new service would be compiled, taking into account the new insights. Those who introduced the Parish Communion into their parishes often made changes in the words of the Prayer Book service, but these were of a minor character. People attending a Parish Communion for the first time were well aware that they were sharing in a service of the Church of England; the ceremonial might be different from anything they had previously experienced but the words were in the familiar language of the Book of Common Prayer. This fact was in itself a living demonstration of one of the chief points which the Liturgical Movement was seeking to make, namely that the Holy Communion is primarily an action, with words added to indicate the meaning of what is taking place. Once this is accepted, the words actually used become far less significant than is commonly supposed, particularly within the Protestant tradition where, in spite of a warning by Jesus, it is still believed that Christians are 'heard for their much speaking'. Nonetheless, it is obviously desirable

[2] *The Parish Communion Today* edited by David M. Paton, p. 138f, SCM Press, 1962.
[3] *Durham Essays and Addresses*, p. 21, SPCK, 1957.

that the words of a liturgy should be appropriate to the
action and, if possible, illuminating. Certainly they should
not obscure the significance of what is happening or be
a cause of disunity among those taking part. Revision of
the Book of Common Prayer could not, therefore, be
long delayed.

In 1954 the Archbishops of Canterbury and York
appointed a Liturgical Commission 'to consider questions
of a liturgical character submitted to them from time
to time by the Archbishops of Canterbury and York'.
Four years later the Commission produced a series of
new services for the administration of Baptism and
Confirmation. These represented a fairly considerable departure from the Prayer Book services – so different that
two members of the Commission felt unable to approve
certain parts of them – and they were given a hostile
reception by the Convocations. In any case, the exercise
was quite academic for even had the services been widely
acclaimed the Church of England had at that time no
authority with which to authorize their use. If anyone
desired to see the new services in action – the only way
in which any liturgy can be assessed – it proved necessary
to borrow a child's doll and simulate a Baptism. The
debates in the Convocations served, however, to remind
any who may have overlooked the point that large
assemblies are not ideal for liturgical drafting. In such
gatherings everyone becomes his own expert, which is
true in the sense that all the members of the church are
involved in and concerned about forms of worship, but
unfortunately few are prepared simply to say: 'I don't
like it.' It is felt necessary to offer historical or theological explanations for this attitude and, since the
overwhelming majority are not adequately equipped in
these fields, the result is grotesque. When the point is
reached at which some hundreds of individuals begin to
propose amendments, ranging from the movement of a
comma to the substitution of a completely new rite, it is
time for reasonable men to consult their railway time-
tables and make for home. The debates on the proposed
Baptism and Confirmation offered a further piece of in-
struction for beginners: discussions of liturgy reveal

more quickly and clearly than anything else fundamental differences in doctrine. Although worship and the sacraments belong by their very nature to the realm of mystery, there is never lacking a body of Christians who claim to know precisely what is happening – and how – and who insist on expressing their unique insights in the liturgical prints so that others may benefit therefrom. Needless to say, they find it virtually impossible to reach agreement among themselves and the church, together with those inhabitants of the world who can be troubled with such things, is then treated to the unedifying spectacle of rival groups locked in conflict and disagreement over a few words which lie at the heart of a Baptismal or eucharistic liturgy.

The consequent pains began to be felt soon after the appearance of the first essay in liturgical revision. They have intensified considerably since 1965 when the membership of the Liturgical Commission was changed and its scope greatly widened. Among a variety of tasks entrusted to the Commission, the most important was, in the words of its terms of reference, 'to assist in the planning and consideration of lawful experiments in forms of service in parishes'. The key word here was 'lawful'. No experimental service could be used lawfully unless Parliament gave it approval and, since neither churchmen nor politicians desired every proposal of the Liturgical Commission to be scrutinized by the House of Commons and the House of Lords, it was decided to seek the approval of Parliament for the church to authorize experimental services for a period of fifteen years. Parliament thankfully approved the Prayer Book (Alternate and Other Services) Measure in 1965 in the expectation that by 1980 the Church of England would have completed a revision of the Prayer Book and be in a position to submit this for Parliamentary consideration. Here it may be noted that no change was envisaged in the post-Reformation legislation by which the church is eventually required to obtain the approval of the State for changes in public worship, though the Measure did give permanent powers to the bishops and Convocations to authorize the use of services on occasions not provided

for in the Book of Common Prayer. The Archbishop
of Canterbury also dropped a broad hint about the out-
come of the 15 year experimental period when he said,
in introducing the Measure in the House of Lords, 'Perhaps by that time church and state may together
have discovered some new means of legislating for future
needs.'[4] Dr. Ramsey was clearly anxious to avoid any
repetition of the 1928 experience, but recognized that
this could not be guaranteed while relations between
church and state remained unchanged. The 1965 Measure
subjected the power temporarily granted to the church
to three important safeguards. (1) New services cannot
supplant those contained in the Book of Common Prayer.
The latter must remain available for use and no new form
of service can be used in any church without the agreement of the parochial church council. (2) Any new form
of service must in the opinion of the Convocations (later
the General Synod) be 'neither contrary to, nor indicative
of any departure from, the doctrine of the Church of
England'. (3) New forms of service must be approved
by two-thirds majorities in each of the three houses of
Bishops, Clergy and Laity in the Church Assembly (later
the General Synod). Restrictions of this kind hardly assist
in the creation of an atmosphere in which dynamic and
adventurous liturgy thrives, but Parliament would not
have approved the proposed period of experiment without
these safeguards and, in any case, the Church of England
was quite happy to offer them.[5]

There now appears to be a good chance that the envisaged revision of the Prayer Book will be completed
by 1980. The Liturgical Commission has worked hard
and produced a number of experimental services which
are well on the way to gaining acceptance. Forms proposed for Morning and Evening Prayer and for The Litany
first appeared in 1962 and are not easily distinguishable
from those compiled by Cranmer in 1549. No one seems

[4] *Hansard,* vol. 263, p. 655.
[5] In November 1972 the General Synod passed the Church of England
(Worship and Doctrine) Measure which, if accepted by Parliament
will give the church permanent power to determine its doctrine and
worship.

greatly concerned about this fact. Those most interested
in liturgical change see little future for these services
anyway; while more conservative parishes remain at
liberty to use the old Prayer Book forms. The services
suggested for the Burial of the Dead are not greatly
different from the modified versions of the 1662 service
produced in 1928 – nor is there any pressing reason why
they should be – but a wider choice of material is offered
and the 20th-century church is still able to fulfil the
hope of the Puritans that it might be possible 'To inter
the corpse in a reverent and decent manner.' Unfortunately, it proved impossible for the Church Assembly
to discuss the new services in a similar manner. The
inclusion of prayers for the dead served to resuscitate
the evangelical corpse which is ever disturbed by the
possibility of Masses for the Dead becoming once again
a part of the daily programme of English parish churches.
That nothing was further from the mind of the Liturgical
Commission, and that the prayers were for optional use
by any who felt moved to pray for their deceased relatives and friends, was considered beside the point. A
doctrinal issue was at stake: What do Christians believe
about the fate of the departed? What does the Church of
England believe about the fate of the departed? In the
absence of clear evidence, it might be thought that a little
reverent agnosticism would not be out of place and that
a certain variety in forms of devotion would not only
be necessary but very desirable. But the evangelical has
little room for agnosticism, only for certainty, and
prefers a bogus certainty to the confession, 'I don't
know.' Those who opposed the inclusion of prayers for
the dead professed to know what had happened to the
departed and where they now were, but fortunately the
majority of Church Assembly members were less sure
and the prayers are now in common use. The evangelicals
were to be placated later by the matter being remitted to
a newly appointed Doctrinal Commission for further consideration, but there was little consolation for them
when this Commission reported in 1971: 'There must be
a considerable liberty in both doctrine and practice
allowed to individual consciences. The status within the

Church of England both of those who find the practice of prayers for the dead theologically acceptable and appropriate, and those who do not, is, of course, not called into question.[6]

New services for Baptism and Confirmation appeared in 1967. These, like their predecessors of 1958, were markedly different from the traditional forms in use and, once again, raised acute theological problems. This time the issue was notably arcane: at what point and on what occasion is the Holy Spirit given to the Christian initiate – is the gift given in Baptism or in Confirmation? Theologians had been debating the question for a couple of decades without reaching a common mind, so the Liturgical Commission, with no little skill, produced services which would neither exclude nor assert exclusively any one of several viewpoints. An evangelical member of the Commission was permitted to say in the official report on the services that he 'would have desired the services more clearly to express that the work of the Spirit in sacramental initiation is complete in Baptism', but they passed into experimental use without too much controversy and appear to be increasingly valued in the churches which use them. Ironically, in 1971 when the services were beginning to become more widely used a new report on Christian initiation appeared and made radical proposals which, if accepted and implemented, would permit the admission of children to Holy Communion prior to Confirmation. The Confirmation service would then become something approaching an ordination or commissioning to adult lay ministry in the church and would not be appropriate until a Christian was about 18 years of age. Thus the process has begun of undermining the long-established view – that Baptism, Confirmation and First Communion are all integral parts of the rite of initiation – which informed the Liturgical Commission's approach to revision. This raises a crucial issue for the Church of England: granted that liturgical change must reflect changes in conviction and experience, how can the process of revision keep pace with the new insights and experiences which are a feature of contemporary

[6] *Prayer and the Departed*, p. 13, SPCK, 1971.

life? If new services are seen to be out of date as soon
as, or soon after, they are produced for experimental use,
the present process of liturgical revision would appear to
be inadequate and a quite different approach called for.

The issue is raised again, and even more urgently, by
the proposals for a new service of Holy Communion. Of
all the work undertaken by the Liturgical Commission,
this has aroused the greatest interest, and for the obvious
reason that it occupies a prominent place on the agendas
of all those parishes where the Holy Communion is the
chief act of worship every Sunday. Two alternative
services (Series 1 and Series 2) were presented to the
Church Assembly in 1966. Series 1 represented a modest
amendment of the service provided in the 1928 Prayer
Book and offered something to those not desiring to
depart from the traditional and well-known form. Series
2, on the other hand, was a major revision and, although
some familiar material was retained from the 1662
service, it was to all intents and purposes a new liturgy. It
reflected the viewpoint of the Liturgical Movement by
strengthening the Ministry of the Word, providing dia-
logue and informal prayer for the Intercession, placing
the Offertory in close proximity to the Prayer of Thanksgiving, including in the Prayer of Thanksgiving a remem-
brance of all the great acts of Creation and Redemption,
and concluding the service with a brief dismissal almost
immediately after the Communion. The use of certain
traditional prayers was considered by some to give the
service an unsatisfactory central section between the
Ministry of the Word and the Offertory but, politically,
it was probably wise to include some familiar material in
view of the extensive changes reflected by the service
as a whole. Predictably, a number of doctrinal issues
came to the fore when the service was presented to the
Church Assembly. The question of prayers for the dead
caused anxiety in evangelical quarters, but the main issue
involved a protracted debate as to whether, and in what
sense, the Holy Communion might be regarded as a sacrifice. This was an old issue, going back as far as the
Reformation and before, and the 1958 Lambeth Conference – somewhat prematurely as it turned out – endorsed

the view of Father Hebert that the conflict was at an end since 'The eucharistic sacrifice, that storm-centre of controversy, is finding in our day a truly evangelical expression from the catholic side.'[7] While this may have been true of professional theologians in 1951, it was certainly not convincing for the evangelical element in the Church Assembly in 1966 and two whole days were spent debating the merits and demerits of seven words in the proposed Prayer of Thanksgiving which attempted to express a view of sacrifice which might be be acceptable to all shades of opinion in the Church of England. The end result was a patched up compromise which completely satisfied no one and led to a poor piece of liturgical drafting. The debate itself can only be described as a nightmare.

Series 2, as it came to be called, was authorized for an experimental period of five years. During this time the views of a cross section of those using the new rite would be canvassed and then collated to provide the basis for any further revision that might be called for. The service is now widely used, especially in the Parish Communion parishes, and after an initial period of questioning has come to be widely appreciated. A revision (Series 3) was published in June 1971 and has now been authorised for use in February 1973. This incorporates minor changes, based on the views obtained from parishes and also on an agreement reached among members of the Liturgical Commission about the best way of dealing with the problem of sacrifice. The most significant change, however, is to be found in the language of the service. Whereas Series 2 had retained the traditional modes of addressing God as 'Thee' and 'Thou' Series 3 is in modern English and uses 'You' forms of prayer. The Liturgical Commission now hopes that Series 3 will become the Church of England's definitive liturgy for some time to come, but it is clear that the chances of the church ever again having just one Communion rite are exceedingly remote. For one thing, the Book of Common Prayer service, in both its 1662 and Series 1

---

[7] *Lambeth Conference Report 1958*: section 2.84, SPCK, 1958.

forms, will remain available for those parishes desiring to use it. And such is the speed with which conservatism establishes itself that already there is a strong desire in some quarters for Series 2 to remain an authorized rite, even though it was produced only for experimental use and intended to prepare the way for something better. The life of Series 2 has now been extended until 1976 and requests have been made – though not so far accepted by the General Synod – that a modern language version should be prepared.

At this point the story of the Church of England's recent liturgical activity might conveniently end, with a few sentences added to express satisfaction at the degree of progress that has been possible during the past quarter of a century. Unfortunately, neither liturgy nor church history is patient of so simple a treatment. The experience of the Church of England in the field of liturgical reform has exposed three questions which now demand the most careful consideration and which constitute a serious, though largely unrecognized, crisis for England's national church. It is possible only to outline these questions in a book of this size and scope, but to neglect them entirely would be to disregard certain issues which may in the long run be decisive in determining the future of the institution under discussion.

The first question enquires whether the Church of England can retain its unity while at the same time allowing, or even encouraging, considerable liturgical diversity. Viewed simply from the angle of the liturgist the answer is an emphatic Yes. Since liturgy is, or should be, derived from life and culture, wide varieties of form must be regarded as a normal feature of a church's life. Christian history shows that diverse liturgies can exist side by side without undue difficulty and sometimes with mutual enrichment. If there has been a problem in this area of the church's life – and most liturgists believe there has – it has been related to lack of variety, rather than over much of it. Yet this presupposes that churches have certain doctrinal standards to which their members adhere and which provide the basis of unity. And this is precisely what the Church of England lacks. While the

churches of the Reformation were labouring over the
production of confessional statements, the Church of
England was preoccupied with the machinations of English politics. Never greatly enamoured of doctrine,
English churchmen concentrated on finding pragmatic
solutions which would enable them to retain as much as
possible of their heritage, while at the same time becoming free to move in certain new directions. Subscription
to the 39 Articles of Religion was exacted of the clergy
from 1571 onwards but, as the Archbishops' Commission on Christian Doctrine point out in their report on the
subject in 1968, 'the doctrinal demands of the Articles
were (in terms of their period) minimal.'[8] It was anticipated, moreover, that the Articles would be interpreted
in the light of the Book of Common Prayer and the
Ordinal : *lex orandi lex credendi*. Hence the development
of a tradition nicely expressed by the 17th-century
scholar John Selden in his *Table Talk* : 'If you would
know how the Church of England serves God, go to the
Common Prayer Book, consult not this or that man'.
Whenever matter concerning doctrinal orthodoxy are
raised, Anglicans are, therefore, inclined to turn to the
Prayer Book to see what may be deduced from the rites,
rubrics and ceremonies enshrined in its closely-packed
pages. If a belief or practice is discovered to be contrary
to the theological standpoint of the Prayer Book, this is
sufficient evidence that it cannot be held by a loyal
member of the Church of England.

This might in some circumstances be convenient, were
it not for the fact that a great many things in the Prayer
Book can be understood and interpreted in very different
ways. Very few of those who use the Communion service
today accept the eucharistic doctrine which Cranmer
sought to express through it. The concepts of original sin
and regeneration which are embedded in the Baptism service have been subjected to considerable reinterpretation
by many Anglicans. Ministry and priesthood, as expressed
in the Prayer Book and the Ordinal, have been, and
are, variously interpreted. Hence the different theological

[8] *Subscription and Assent to the 39 Articles*, p. 10, SPCK, 1968.

standpoints which find a home within Anglican comprehensiveness. Yet all share common ground in
their acceptance of the Prayer Book and their use of it,
in some form or another, in regular worship. If this
common ground is removed, or at least severely shaken,
by the authorization of many different liturgical rites,
some of which are quite different from others, will it be
possible for the fragile unity of the Church of England to
be maintained? Is it not likely that the use of differing
rites over a long period will isolate those who hold particular doctrinal positions and, in the end, cause fragmen-
tation? Stated another way, if liturgy ceases to be the
cement binding the Church of England together, what
will take its place? The risk of division is not in itself a
good enough reason for trying to limit that liturgical
creativity which finds expression in a diversity of rites,
but it is an excellent reason for considering the basis
of the Church of England's unity in a time of liturgical
and theological fluidity.

The next question involves the exceedingly complex
and subtle areas of symbolism, language and tradition.
The fact that the Book of Common Prayer was allowed to
survive more or less unchanged for over four centuries is
frequently deplored, and it is fair to say that if the
Church of England had been a vigorous body it would,
certainly by the end of the 18th century, have sought
permission to revise its forms of worship. Yet four centuries of continuous use have served to burn something
of the ethos and language of the Prayer Book into the
corporate memory of the English nation. When the words
are those of the most creative era in English language and
literature, the evocative effects are often deeper than is
commonly recognized. Whatever asset this represents
may well be a wasting one as succeeding generations
become further removed from the community in which
this particular element in the nation's corporate memory
is kept alive. Yet those who still come to the Church of
England on the occasion of a Baptism, a Marriage or a
Burial – they are a large proportion of the country's
population – find that the words and phrases of the
Book of Common Prayer ring bells of one kind and

another in their consciousness. What this amounts to in terms of spirituality and insight is obviously impossible to tell. It may be no more than sentiment or vague folk memory. But something so intangible, yet so common, cannot lightly be dismissed or cast aside, least of all by a church which still claims to represent in some sense the spiritual dimension of the English nation as a whole. Dr. R. C. D. Jasper, the chairman of the Liturgical Commission, is a late convert to the use of modern English in liturgical texts. For several years he resolutely withstood all suggestions that contemporary English should be used in Anglican worship and both spoke and wrote of the importance of hieratic language in liturgy. But now, in the light of experience and as a result of working with liturgists of other churches in the International Consultation on English Texts, Dr. Jasper is happy to use modern language and 'You' forms of prayer. Modern versions of all the new services are now in course of preparation.

Strange as it may seem, Dr. Jasper's conversion coincided with a pause for second thoughts by some of those who had been most vocal in demanding the use of contemporary English and who had often accused the members of the Liturgical Commission of dragging their feet. Their viewpoint, and that of many of a more conservative disposition, was expressed with great clarity by the Dean of Guildford (the Very Revd. A. C. Bridge) in a memorable speech at the General Synod in November 1971. Well known for his radical views on a variety of subjects, the Dean is a former professional painter and retains great interest in artistic and religious symbolism. He began his speech by informing the Synod that a liturgical rite was more closely related to an epic poem or a Shakespeare play than to a piece of straight prose. He believed that a committee could no more be expected to produce a new liturgy than they could be expected to write a poem or become joint authors of a new *Hamlet*. This was an age of literary infertility and linguistic poverty, so it was not surprising that a latter-day Cranmer had not emerged. Hence the new Series 3 service was full of false archaisms – biblical phrases, biblical

ideas re-expressed, and archaic doctrinal ideas semi-
reclothed in contemporary words. Turning to the suggestion that the traditional language no longer com-
municated and stamped the church as an antique relic
of the past, Dean Bridge replied, 'What nonsense this is!
In a comparable case, no one is presently suggesting that
Shakespeare or the Restoration dramatists are out of date,
and that their language no longer communicates, or that
the Old Vic is an antique relic to which no one wishes to
go any more. On the contrary, they have never been
more popular – and not least among young people. I am
not denying that more and more people seem to find
formal liturgical worship incomprehensible and irrelevant.
But I am denying that new liturgies framed in the
language of semi-contemporary prose of dubious distinc-
tion will make formal worship any more significant to a
single person.' The Dean's point has yet to be answered,
and there can be no adequate discussion of this point
until liturgists and theologians have paid attention to
recent research into the sociology of languages and begun
to consider the place of symbolism in corporate worship.
It is therefore a little early for the Church of England
to throw away its poetic and linguistic heritage from the
past, though it may in the end be right for it to do so.

Dean Bridge's introductory comment on the difficulty
of a committee producing a liturgy raises the third question: Is the Church of England approaching liturgical
reform from the wrong end? Christian worship is the
means by which a group of people in a particular place
express their devotion to God. Since people vary very
considerably in outlook, temperament and culture, it is
to be anticipated that these variations will be reflected in
their forms of worship. It would be surprising if an
African in a Nigerian village chose to worship in exactly
the same way as an Englishman in a Sussex village,
though such was the power of the 19th-century missionary imperialism that many Africans have in fact been
obliged to adjust their outlook to that of the Book of
Common Prayer. Variety in liturgy is therefore to be
regarded as normal, and uniformity highly suspect; hence
the depressing character of the closing words of Cranmer's

preface to the Prayer Book: 'And whereas heretofore there hath been great diversity in saying and singing in churches within this realm; some following Salisbury use, some Hereford use, and some the use of Bangor, some of York, some of Lincoln; now from henceforth all of the whole realm shall have but one use.' It is clear why Cranmer and other leaders of church and state required uniformity in the 16th century, and it is also apparent that any significant departure from liturgical uniformity raises doctrinal problems in a church that has no independent confession of faith. But this does not absolve the Church of England from paying attention to certain fundamental questions about the nature of liturgy, in particular, whether forms of worship must develop out of local situations, experiences and needs, rather than be compiled in a London committee room and then be required to run the gauntlet of a 600-member General Synod? The present Liturgical Commission is a highly competent body to handle a London-based programme of revision, but it might well be better employed in advising groups of Christians in dioceses and parishes who wish to try their hand at devising forms of worship for local use and in attempting to co-ordinate the results.

There is irony – and surely significance – in the fact that, while the Series 3 Communion service meets all the demands which the younger generation of reformers were making in the late 1950s and early 1960s, these same people no longer regard the new service as relevant to their personal needs or to the situations in which they are now working. The emphasis now is on informality and spontaneity. Groups of Christians, from all traditions, meeting in homes and other non-ecclesiastical premises find themselves unable to make meaningful use of any of the official liturgies of their churches, so they devise their own. These vary in quality, as might be expected, and too many of them seem to be addressed to the assembled company rather than to God, but among the very large – and increasing – output of homespun services there are a number which travel quite well from their places of origin to other locations and gatherings. When this activity and its results are compared with the General

Synod's debates on liturgical matters it is not difficult
to discern where the real liturgical creativity is now to
be found. Neither can this comparatively recent development be isolated from the deep concern for celebration,
in many different forms, which is one of the chief
characteristics of the younger generation in the country
as a whole. The 'pop festival', the 'folk festival' and the
various musical and dramatic occasions which are bringing young people together in large numbers bear many
of the marks of true liturgy and from the religious, as
well as the sociological, point of view are of the greatest
significance.

The uncomfortable question facing the Church of England is whether all its recent efforts in the field of liturgical reform will succeed in restoring worship to a place
where it is expressive of the life of a living human
community or whether Anglican liturgy, in company
with that of the Roman Catholic Church, is now condemned to a position akin to that of the liturgies of the
Orthodox churches where the worship is ancient, mys-
terious, beautiful and moving, yet utterly remote from the
daily lives of the worshippers. The answer to this question will determine the place which the Church of
England is to have in the life of the English nation in the
centuries to come.

chapter 6

Beauty in Bands

In the sermon preached at his enthronement as Archbishop of Canterbury in 1961, Dr. Michael Ramsey gave a clear indication that he hoped to see some modification in the relationship between the Church of England and the state during his time as Primate of All England. Eleven years later, time appears to be running out on the Archbishop for the position is precisely the same now as it was when Prime Minister Harold Macmillan nominated him to the Queen for the highest appointment in the Established Church. But Dr. Ramsey is not the first – nor is he likely to be the last – archbishop to be frustrated in his hope of being able to disentangle certain elements in the organization of the church from the power structure of the state. During the present century five Church of England commissions have considered the subject in some depth and produced certain proposals for change. Other commissions met in the previous century. All of which suggests that a number of influential people are less than happy with the present arrangements. Yet these continue along their well worn paths. Archbishops and other Anglican dignitaries still officiate at state ceremonies requiring the blessing of the church. The announcements of their appointments still come from No. 10 Downing Street. Evidently the reformers are neither numerous nor influential enough to secure change, or maybe change is impossible.

One thing is certain: if church and state were starting their lives *de novo* in the 20th century, no one would dream of suggesting any relationship between the two even remotely resembling that which currently exists, and even if he did no one would dream of taking him seriously. But neither church nor state is starting *de novo*.

and herein lies the problem. History does not easily yield to those who are seeking to change something which has been accepted, and for the most part valued, for more than a thousand years. It is commonly believed that the establishment of the Church of England was one of the more dubious results of the 16th-century Reformation: Henry VIII and all that. But this is a serious mistake. The Church of England's position in English society may be traced back to 597 when Augustine arrived in Kent and on Whitsunday of that year baptized King Ethelbert at Canterbury. Soon afterwards Augustine became Archbishop of the English. William of Normandy found the church well organized when he conquered England in the 11th century and both convenience and conviction required him to integrate his government with that of the church. Throughout the Middle Ages the relationship was maintained. Crown nominees held high office in the church; bishops held high office in the state. No one thought to question this, since the fabric of church and society were interwoven at every level. At the Reformation, therefore, this long-established situation was simply given formal recognition. The state recognized the Church of England as an integral part of national life and afforded it the protection of law. The church's own laws had been upheld, and where necessary enforced, by the state for several centuries, but the severing of links with Rome provided an opportunity for the relationship between church and state to be reassessed and codified in new forms. That the situation in 20th-century England is quite different from that which obtained in the 11th and 16th centuries lies beyond dispute, yet the nation still regards itself as in some sense Christian (at both the corporate and personal levels) and the Church of England still regards itself as having some responsibility for the well-being of the nation. Given the history of the relationship and the elements of it which remain, it is far from easy to think in terms of a complete divorce, even though a good deal of the reality has been eroded by the growth of secularism and the church has become increasingly conscious of itself as an autonomous society.

Examined from the point of view of the Church of England, the present establishment offers a number of privileges and opportunities. Not all are of equal value, and those who would like to see changes in the relationship argue that the church ought not, in any case, to accept a privileged position in society. Be that as it may, it is possible to identify certain factors in the establishment which place the Church of England in a position different from that of the other English churches. At a Coronation it is the Archbishop of Canterbury who crowns the Sovereign as Head of the State. The Sovereign must be a communicant member of the Church of England. The Archbishops of Canterbury and York, together with the Bishops of London, Durham and Winchester and 21 other diocesan bishops (in seniority of appointment) have seats in the House of Lords. A bishop conducts daily prayers in the House of Lords and the Speaker's chaplain, who must be a priest of the Church of England, conducts prayers in the House of Commons. On national occasions requiring religious rites and ceremonies the clergy of the Church of England are given precedence over the priests and ministers of other churches. Similarly in the institutions of the state, Church of England clergy provide the official religious ministry, leaving other churches simply to minister to their own members. The 'parson's freehold', which entitles a Church of England clergyman to remain in a parish until death or voluntary resignation, is part of English law and a priest can only be removed by means of a process recognized by the state. A number of academic appointments in the Universities of Oxford, Cambridge and Durham are restricted to clergymen of the Church of England. Those who value the establishment believe some, or all, of these arrangements to be important and would regret their disappearance. But their concern for the maintenance of the establishment springs, in the main, from less tangible considerations. The particular privileges given to the Church of England are seen as expressions of a deep relationship between the church and the nation, and it is the severance of this relationship that they would most regret.

The price which the Church of England is required to pay for its privileges is a heavy one. All its chief officers – archbishops, bishops and cathedral deans – are appointed by the Crown, acting on the advice of the Prime Minister. All matters relating to changes in the Church of England's worship or reinterpretations of its doctrine are subject to the approval of Parliament. Many other administrative matters, e.g. creation or abolition of dioceses, clergy pensions, parsonage houses, etc., require the agreement of Parliament before they can be implemented. A Church of England clergyman is not allowed to stand for Parliament, or, to be more precise, he cannot take a seat in the House of Commons if elected. When church and society were completely integrated in England these arrangements were logical and agreeable. That the church should be given a prominent place in the affairs of the nation was not regarded as an imposition, or even as a privilege, by a population whose own life was deeply influenced by the Christian faith and the corporate witness of the Christian community. Neither was the involvement of the state in church government regarded as an imposition. Parliament represented the mind of the Church of England's laity and its power of veto over the proposals of the Convocations was a useful safeguard against the clericalism which had destroyed the unity of the mediaeval church. Even the nomination of bishops by the Crown was defensible on the grounds that their office required them to be servants of the whole community and not simply leaders of an ecclesiastical body which might in certain circumstances be tempted to dominate and sacralize society or, alternatively, withdraw into sectarianism.

This position held good so long as England was overtly a Christian nation. Once the development of the scientific outlook and the growth of industrialization had begun to eat into the traditional beliefs of the people, it was inevitable that church and state should grow apart. The process has been a slow one because Englishmen are not generally inclined to favour revolutionary changes in the structure of their society, but by the end of the 19th century strains on the establishment were beginning to make themselves felt and could not long be ignored. From the Church of England's point of view, it was, to say the least, inappropriate that Members of Parliament who were not members of the church, and in some instances not even Christian, should be in a position to prevent the church from making changes in forms of worship and doctrinal expression. The chances of appointments to bishoprics being determined solely by political, rather than religious, considerations were obviously increased. There was a further point, which has become more prominent as the process of secularization has continued throughout the years of the 20th century: does not the establishment of the church give a totally misleading impression of the religious state of the nation? By maintaining an essentially mediaeval arrangement, the impression is given that the religious situation which originated and sustained the intimate link between church and state still exists, whereas in fact only the empty husk of the old national piety remains. So the argument has run for 70 years, and those who were becoming anxious about the possibility of state interference in ecclesiastical affairs had their worst fears confirmed when Parliament rejected the Prayer Books of 1927 and 1928. Writing of Cosmo Gordon Lang's appointment to Canterbury, soon after the rejection of the Prayer Book, Dr. Hensley Henson, then Bishop of Durham, commented gloomily: 'He comes to his throne at an evil time. Since Cranmer's accession was there ever a darker outlook for the Church of England?'

But there was a problem for the state, too. As the growth of modern society advanced, Parliament was required to devote more and more of its time to important legislation which it was hoped would improve the social and economic conditions of the nation. The controversy surrounding the revised Prayer Book had caused a great deal of interest at the time, but few Members of Parliament wished to devote their time and energy to debating ecclesiastical affairs and there were many urgent matters to keep them occupied throughout the 1930s. So a characteristically English solution to the church-state problem was reached, or rather evolved with the passage

of time. No official negotiations took place, but certain
things began to be taken for granted and blind eyes were
turned when former customs and prerogatives were conveniently forgotten. Parliament made no further attempts
to veto ecclesiastical legislation which had been approved
by the Church Assembly. The 1928 Prayer Book began
to be used in parish churches, with the tacit agreement
of the bishops, and Parliament recognized that, while it
had power to withhold official recognition from the
Church of England's forms of worship, it could do nothing
to stop them from being used. The church, for its part,
recognized the need to work in close co-operation with
Parliamentary lawyers when drafting legislation in order
to become better acquainted with the sensitivities of
Government ministers and M.Ps. who are concerned to
maintain the rights and freedoms of those whom they
represent. Hence the present position in which church
and state maintain a peaceful coexistence; neither being
particularly anxious to bring the establishment to an
end, yet each emphatic in its rejection of interference by
the other in affairs which are of particular ecclesiastical
or governmental concern. So successful has been the
compromise, that establishment no longer seems objec-
tionable in principle even to the English Free churches.
For many years Free churchmen were among the fore-
most advocates of disestablishment, partly because they
objected to the privileges which it offered to the Church
of England, but mainly because they believed that the
Church of God should not in any way be compromised
in its relations with a secular institution. But by the time
Methodists had become involved in serious conversation
with Anglicans in the 1960s it was possible for the joint
commission to say, 'We believe that the majority of both
Free Churchmen and Anglicans see more clearly how
desirable it is to retain a positive partnership between the
church and the state, less perhaps for the church's sake
than for the state's. And this is likely to be, not less,
but more true when the united church comes into being.'[1]
True, the Methodists were taking for granted certain

[1] *Anglican Methodist Unity*, 2 The Scheme, p. 98, SPCK and
Epworth Press, 1968.

important modifications in the present arrangement between the state and the Church of England, but even over
the thorny question of appointments they were ready to
recognize the need for 'a procedure whereby bishops
and principal officers may be appointed by the united
church in such a way that they will be recognized by
the state and the nation.'[2]

Crown appointments to bishoprics and deaneries is
now the one aspect of the establishment which most –
though by no means all – churchmen believe to be in
urgent need of change. A certain difficulty is encountered
here, however, since no one is quite clear how these
appointments are made. At one time there was much less
obscurity. The first Elizabeth wrote to one diocesan
bishop:

Proud Prelate,

You know what you were before I made you what
you now are. If you do not immediately comply with my
request, I will unfrock you, by God.

ELIZABETH

Such a letter helps to clarify the issues admirably, and
although most of Elizabeth's successors have been less
forthright, they were, at least until the present century,
deeply interested in episcopal appointments and played
an important part in choosing men for an office which
was influential not only in the church but also in the
state. When a new Archbishop of Canterbury was needed
in 1805, the Prime Minister (Pitt) recommended George
Pretyman Tomline (then Bishop of Lincoln) for the position, but as soon as George III received the letter he rode
over to Windsor and immediately offered the job to his
close friend Manners Sutton, who had combined the
Bishopric of Norwich with the Deanery of Windsor since
1794. Queen Victoria spent a good deal of her time
suggesting and vetting names for church appointments.
When Disraeli wished to appoint Bishop Ellicott of
Gloucester to the Archbishopric of Canterbury in 1868,

[2] *ibid*, p. 99.

D

the Queen expressed a preference for Bishop Tait of London. Tait was appointed. The church's involvement in decision-making was restricted to the careful advice tended to the Queen by successive Deans of Windsor. Dean Wellesley was her adviser for 28 years and was followed by Randall Davidson, himself destined to become Archbishop of Canterbury. Five years after the death of Queen Victoria, Davidson wrote a memorandum describing the way in which the system worked:

The Queen's usage was this; when an ecclesiastical post of any importance – a bishopric, a deanery, sometimes even a canonry – was vacant, the Queen would ask me to advise her as to the sort of man who ought to hold such a position. About this she took a really continuous interest and did not like to wait until a recommendation should arrive from the Prime Minister before forming opinions of her own about the vacant position and the sort of man who was to fill it . . . Sometimes I advised her to accept nominations which did not seem to me very good ones, but I never scrupled to advise her to veto nominations if they were really unsuitable or bad, and during my years of advising her the veto was exercised a great many times.[3]

Later, when he became Archbishop of Canterbury, Davidson expressed his view of the Prime Minister's role in the making of ecclesiastical appointments in a letter to Lord Parmoor, following a meeting with the then Prime Minister (David Lloyd George) in Parmoor's house in January 1924. He wrote:

The Prime Minister's nominations to the Crown must be based on adequate information which he has obtained in such a way as he thinks best. The procedure he follows in obtaining that information is of his own planning and carrying out, and the Crown has, so to speak, no direct concern in it, but simply receives from the Prime Minister advice which is based on the Prime Minister's own enquiries. The Prime Minister may courteously tell us privately that the procedure he means to follow is the consulting of the two Archbishops and some others, but, if I may say so, I think that the Sovereign should have no *official* cognizance of this, but

[3] *Randall Davidson* by G. K. A. Bell, p. 164, Oxford University Press, 3rd edition, 1952.

should simply receive the nominations as coming from a well-informed Prime Minister.[4]

Four years earlier Davidson had strongly resisted a proposal by the Lower House of the Convocation of Canterbury that the Prime Minister should be officially required to consult the two Archbishops before making nominations, though in fact it was by then normal practice for the Prime Minister to consult them and a number of other prominent churchmen before submitting names to the King.

More recently, Winston Churchill's reluctance to appoint William Temple to Canterbury in 1942, because of his socialist leanings, is well known. But Churchill had no real choice in the matter because Temple was the outstanding candidate and the wartime Prime Minister is alleged to have remarked, grumpily: 'He is the only sixpenny article in a penny bazaar'. As it happened Churchill did not have to suffer his equal for long, and the diary of Sir Alexander Cadogan, secretary of the Cabinet during the war years, contains a revealing entry: 'Thursday, 26 October 1944. News came of death of Archbishop of Canterbury. P.M. delighted'. Nor was Churchill prepared to be trapped again. After an inordinately long delay, which Archbishop Garbett of York described as scandalous, it was announced from Downing Street that the new occupant of the throne of St. Augustine was to be Bishop Fisher of London. Thus was by-passed the most able member of the bench of bishops at that time – George Bell of Chichester – whose courageous speeches in the House of Lords opposing the obliteration bombing of Germany will find a place in the annals of Anglican history long after Fisher's supervision of the reform of Canon Law has been thankfully forgotten. Whether Bell would have made a good Archbishop of Canterbury is still disputed by those who knew him best, but it is clear that Churchill would, in the circumstances, have never tolerated his appointment and, in the light of the post-war history of the Church of England, it is becoming even clearer that Professor Donald

[4] *ibid*, p. 1252.

Mackinnon was near the truth when he wrote in 1963:
'The historians of the Church of England may yet recognize that the worst misfortune to befall its leadership in
the end of the war was less the premature death of
William Temple than his succession by Fisher of London,
and not by Bell of Chichester'.[5] When the time came for
Fisher to retire in 1961 the assistance of the Queen
proved to be necessary in deciding upon his successor.
Fisher recommended that Dr. Donald Coggan, then Bishop
of Bradford, should move to Lambeth, but this caused
considerable alarm among the more perceptive members
of the episcopal bench who believed that Michael
Ramsey of York (a former pupil of Fisher's at Repton)
was the only serious runner. The Prime Minister
(Harold Macmillan) informed the Queen of the division
of opinion and is said to have received the constitutionally
proper response: 'Let the senior man have it.' So Ramsey
was translated to Canterbury and Coggan to York –
appointments which prompted *The Times* to congratulate
the Prime Minister in his Trollopian sensitivity in providing a high churchman for one archbishopric and a low
churchman for the other. Little did the leader writer
know of the circumstances which had led to the choices.

Obviously, there is ample ammunition here for those
who are opposed to the present system of appointing the
chief officers in that part of the Body of Christ known as
the Church of England. When consideration is given to
the actual machinery which leads to the making of
nominations the grounds for their disquiet are scarcely
weakened. The Howick Commission, reporting in 1963,
offered a more detailed description of the procedure than
had hitherto been available:

As soon as it is known that a see is vacant or will shortly
become vacant, the Prime Minister's Secretary for Appointments undertakes a series of consultations with the laity as
well as with bishops and other clergy both within and outside the diocese. The widest possible information is sought
and obtained in regard to the needs of the diocese as well as
of the church as a whole. This enquiry is made against the
background of a continuous process of consultation and col-

5 *Theology*, March, 1963.

lation. Only thus can the Prime Minister exercise properly his personal responsibility for the nomination he makes to the Sovereign. Both at an early and at a late stage the respective Archbishop is consulted and the Archbishop of Canterbury is kept informed of developments in both provinces. At the final stage, the respective Archbishop gives the Prime Minister the names of two or three persons, indicating that the choice of any one of them would have his approval. (It will be understood that the names are names of persons whom the Archbishop knows, from the Prime Minister's Appointments Secretary, to be under serious consideration at that stage.) The Prime Minister who has at his disposal all the information afforded by the process of consultation is then in a position to consider his recommendation to the Sovereign for election by the dean and chapter.[6]

No one could doubt the thoroughness of such a procedure, nor the care taken by all who might be involved in it. It was sufficient to convince Lord Howick of Glendale, GCMG, KCVO, the Rt. Hon. Sir Henry Willinck, Bt. and the other twelve commissioners appointed by the Archbishops of Canterbury and York that the procedure was the best possible, though they did recommend that the initiative in the choice of those to be consecrated as bishops should be with the church and that the dioceses should be more closely involved in the consultations. They also suggested that the Archbishops should have a secretary specially concerned with appointments who would maintain records of possible candidates for episcopal office.

These recommendations, which required neither legislation nor the official co-operation of the state, were soon put into effect. In Mr. W. Saumerez Smith the Archbishops have an appointments secretary whose discretion is matched only by the warmth and friendliness of his personality. Based, strategically some would aver, at Cuddesdon, he travels the country unawares, putting in regular appearances at the General Synod but generally leading the life appropriate to a private detective. Since the subjective element cannot be eliminated from assessments of individuals, there are obvious risks in entrusting

[6] *Crown Appointments and the Church*, p. 31, Church Information Office, 1964.

a task of this sort to one man, but given the present basic
appointments system, it must be accounted an improvement on simply trusting the memory of the two Archbishops and there are several other channels of information
available for cross-reference. Among these is the Vacancy-
in-See Committee which is now formed in every diocese
whenever a new diocesan bishop is required. This normally meets under the chairmanship of the suffragan
bishop and is made up of representatives of the clergy
and laity of the diocese. Its task is to prepare a statement
on the needs of the diocese for consideration by the
Prime Minister and the Archbishops. While the committee
is expected to concentrate on the sort of person it believes
the diocese to need, it is not forbidden to mention names
and, in fact, some of the committees have asked for –
and been given – a named individual. Two problems have,
however, already begun to emerge from these committees.
It is observable that they have a tendency to seek the
elevation of a suffragan bishop from either their own
or a neighbouring diocese. This is understandable. There
are limits to the number of men who can be known by
a diocesan committee and among those who may have
caught the approving eye of several members there is
always likely to be an active and popular suffragan
bishop who is already exercising the episcopal office in
the neighbourhood. To opt for such a man, in preference
to some unknown figure (possibly of an academic background) from another part of the country, will seem to
some merely common prudence. Among the ranks of the
suffragan bishops there are many excellent men, some of
whom ought certainly to be entrusted with greater responsibility. But it is a fact that suffragan bishops are not
normally recruited from among the most able priests in
the Church of England. The reasons are not difficult to
find. A suffragan bishopric can be an exceedingly reward-
ing job for a man of pastoral disposition and some administrative ability. But its responsibilities are limited
and are unlikely to appeal to men with academic gifts
who may well be carrying heavier responsibilities in
universities, theological colleges or cathedral posts. If,
therefore, diocesan bishops are recruited from the ranks

of the suffragans too frequently, the dioceses themselves and the bench of bishops as a whole will be lacking in first-class minds.

The second problem arises from the way in which the advice and wishes of the Vacancy-in-See Committee are treated by those who in the end are responsible for making an appointment. Few things are better able to undermine confidence than to seek advice and then, without explanation, announce a decision which appears to run contrary to the views expressed. This has happened in a number of instances since the opinions of dioceses were sought and has caused some cynicism about the new procedure. Norwich is a case in point. Following the resignation in 1970 of Dr. Launcelot Fleming, after a remarkably creative episcopate in an area of East Anglia where the Church of England has been, and still is, faced with its most acute rural problems, a Norwich Vacancy-in-See Committee was called upon to produce a 'specification' for its new bishop. Naturally, it hoped for a man who would be acceptable in parishes of varying shades of theological opinion and who would be able to discern the changing role of the church in a changing rural society. His ability to enter into the problems of priests who are often working in isolated and difficult situations and to give them good leadership and support was equally important. Another, comparatively new, factor in Norwich is the inauguration of the University of East Anglia: it might be expected that the bishop would have a good relationship with the academic staff and the students of a modern university. Considerable disappointment was felt, therefore, when it was announced that the new bishop was to be Prebendary Maurice Wood, a conservative evangelical with a somewhat 'dated' approach to Christian mission, whose entire ministry, apart from a spell as a naval chaplain, had been spent in cities – rector of St. Ebbe, Oxford, vicar of Islington and, most recently, principal of the evangelical theological college at Oak Hill, London. The explanation? There was need for the evangelical voice to be represented on the bench of bishops, so certain local considerations had to be over-ridden. A similar situation had arisen in

Birmingham in 1969, when a successor was needed for
the famous Bishop Leonard Wilson. Here the need was
for a man who could make his presence felt in Britain's
second largest city which presented the Church of England with almost every conceivable 20th-century problem – urban decay, a massive immigrant population, an
important secular university and many hard-pressed
parishes where clergy and small congregations were fighting what appeared to be a losing battle. The call went
out for one of the most able men the church could produce. It is no insult to the man who was appointed to
say that he did not measure up to local requirements.
Perhaps Birmingham was looking for the impossible, or,
at least, for someone who did not exist? Maybe Bishop
Laurence Brown was the best man available? He had
been a popular suffragan Bishop of Warrington, had
successfully piloted The Pastoral Measure through the
Church Assembly (no mean feat) and was now Chairman
of the key Advisory Council on the Church's Ministry.
There was no doubting his outstanding administrative
competence. But why present Birmingham with a pastoral
administrator when it was looking for a prophet? The
answer seems to be that Bishop Brown's considerable
contribution to the central government of the Church of
England now required him to become a diocesan bishop
in order that he might attend the regular bishops' meeting and be available when questions of high policy were
under discussion. Again, the needs of the church as a
whole had been given priority over local requirements.
Obviously this must happen from time to time, since
bishops belong to the whole church, not just to their own
dioceses, but, in the absence of any machinery for com-
municating the reasons for appointments to those most
closely concerned, it is inevitable that some Vacancy-in-
See Committees should feel they have been badly treated.

Of the five reports on church-state relations produced
in the present century, the latest (1970) is by far the
best. The Commission spent four years on its project
– so lengthy a period of gestation that many wondered
whether its progeny might in the end be stillborn – but
Professor Owen Chadwick, its learned chairman, was

faced with the difficult task of keeping together in creative tension such fundamentally incompatible personalities as the Bishop of Leicester and Miss Valerie Pitt. The quality of the report testifies to his success. Having examined the obvious alternatives to the present arrangement (1) a total severing of the historic links, and (2) a form of establishment similar to that which obtains in Scotland, where the Church of Scotland enjoys the status of the national church but retains complete autonomy in its own life, thirteen of the sixteen members of the Commission concluded that (1) would be impracticable because of the present state of public opinion in England, even though it might be desirable from the church's point of view – which the Commission did not believe to be the case, and (2) would be impossible because of the important differences between the English and Scottish situations. The evidence for the view that the majority of Englishmen do not wish to see the Church of England disestablished is somewhat scanty and the Report simply infers that, because the majority of the population still regards themselves as 'C. of E.' and frequent the church for Baptisms, marriages and funerals, 'they are not likely to be pleased by legislation which might suggest that the English people as a whole were going unchristian.'[7] The basis for the opinion that a Scottish-type arrangement is impossible in England appears to be drawn from the reasoning of the Howick Report which pointed out that the policy of the Church of Scotland does not require the appointment of permanent senior officers like bishops and, furthermore, the state could only be expected to give the Church of England spiritual freedom provided it were prepared to adopt a statement of faith, doctrine and constitution similar to that accepted by the Church of Scotland in the Declaratory Articles scheduled to the Church of Scotland Act 1921.[8]

Nonetheless, the Commission recognized the need for change and opined that 'a significant proportion of thinking people in this country would accept the proposition

---

[7] *Church and State: Report of the Archbishops' Commission*, p. 65, Church Information Office, 1970.
[8] *Howick Report*, p. 40.

that the Church of England ought to stand further apart from the State than it now does.' In an attempt to assist such a movement, the Commission made five principal recommendations. All matters affecting the worship and doctrine of the church should become subject to the final authority of the General Synod, with certain safeguards provided. These safeguards would be designed to ensure that new forms of worship are not contrary to the doctrines expressed in the Book of Common Prayer and that they are approved by a two-thirds majority in each of the three houses of the General Synod. When a new diocesan bishop is required an Electoral Board, representing both the diocese concerned and the church at large, should be formed to present the church's view. At this point the Commission was divided on the role of the Electoral Board. Some members thought that it should advise the Crown on the names of persons, through the Prime Minister, but leave the final choice to the Crown; in other words, leave the present system more or less unchanged. Others thought that the Board should elect the bishop and present his name directly to the Sovereign for confirmation; this represents a radical change and apparently overlooks the constitutional problem which would arise from the Sovereign acting without the advice of the Prime Minister. The Commission then turned to the appointment of suffragan bishops, who are at present officially appointed by the Crown but are in fact nominated by the bishop of the diocese in which they are to serve. This arrangement has not been altogether satisfactory, so it was recommended that the choice of suffragan bishops should be made by the proposed Electoral Board (working under either of two suggested systems), with the proviso that no one should be nominated without the consent of the diocesan bishop concerned. The position of bishops in the House of Lords is not easy to discuss at the present time since the future composition of the Upper House of Parliament is uncertain, so the Commission contented itself by recommending that some bishops should always be given seats and that leading members of other churches should be invited by the Government to join them. All clergy and ministers should be free to stand as candidates for Parliament and to take seats in the House of Commons if elected.

A series of recommendations along these lines might well appear to be a reasonable compromise, appealing to the majority of churchmen and politicians alike. If adequately implemented, they would give the Church of England almost complete freedom without severing the historic link between church and state. But the Commission's majority viewpoint was subjected to a searching critique by Miss Valerie Pitt who felt unable to sign the Report and contributed a Memorandum of Dissent. Miss Pitt is a highly literate, and somewhat complex, character whose religious beliefs may be broadly identified with the high church wing of the Church of England. She is deeply aware of the church as a divine society which owes its origin and life to Christ, to whom it is united in sacrament, prayer and service. The autonomy and integrity of the church must therefore never be compromised by too close an association or identification with the 'principalities and powers' which do not share its unique relationship with Christ. It was inevitable that anyone holding these beliefs would have very serious reservations about any form of establishment of the church, and Miss Pitt's Memorandum is a fine exposition of an approach which is shared by many other Anglicans. Her initial disagreement with the majority of the Commission's members concerns the degree to which the proposed reforms would give the church real freedom. While conceding that they would offer a good deal of freedom if church-state relations were cordial, Miss Pitt pointed out that the legal apparatus of the establishment would be left intact and so the state would retain the power to interfere in church affairs if it chose to do so. Such a risk ought not to be taken. But the main thrust of her argument concerned the basic premises on which the Commission's recommendations were built.

The first of these involves a discussion of whether the Church of England any longer represents the folk religion of the nation. Miss Pitt is certain that very little folk religion remains – at least, not in urban areas where the overwhelming majority of the English people are now to be found — and that, in any case, Christianity is not a folk or tribal religion : 'It is a gospel, a revealed religion, demanding an active and personal assent. To be a Christian a man must himself answer — Jesus is Lord. Writing "C. of E." on a form is not quite enough.'[9] Futhermore, to cling to something which is now outside the experience of millions of people would cause the church to identify faith not merely with culture but with a dying culture. The choice before the church, according to Miss Pitt, is between the past and the future and if the church is to exercise its functions properly the whole apparatus of the establishment must be dismantled. This would not lead to the withdrawal of the church from the national life or from its service of the community since the church's vocation is not a matter of law or legal status : 'The identity and coherence of the church will in the long run be discovered and realized in the *ecclesiae*, the local communities of Christians. What we desperately need now are ways and structures which will help to build those local and limited allegiances into the catholic order of the whole Body of Christ. In the present church-state relationship this is impossible for it is itself a relationship between centralized authorities : the Crown, Parliament and the central institutions of the church. These links have to be modified, broken, before the church can in any way begin to release, or to feel within its structures the energies of its "ordinary" congregations.'[10] In another dissenting note, the Revd. Peter Cornwell questioned whether the privileged position, given to the church by establishment, could be justified. He thought not; the church should 'rediscover its own identity and commend its faith without privileged status', and he pointed out that the present generation does not accept institutions which seem to be kept in existence by the props of external authority.

The Church of England is therefore now faced with a decision as to whether it will continue to work within the framework of the present establishment or seek

[9] *Church and State*, p. 74.
[10] *ibid*, p. 79.

modifications along the lines suggested by the Majority Report or go all out for disestablishment. The latter can, for the time being anyway, be completely ruled out. If the state attempted to repeat the performance of 1928 in matters concerning worship and doctrine, or if the appointment of bishops were subjected to political rather than ecclesiastical considerations, there can be no doubt that the overwhelming majority of Anglicans would press for immediate disestablishment. They are already aware that the other churches of the Anglican Communion have expressed their disquiet that the Church of England's bishops are nominated by the Crown. But while anything approaching a church-state confrontation is avoided, the number of people anxious for radical change is likely to be limited. Those who are sympathetic to Miss Pitt's social and theological analysis will also be aware that the church-state link is by no means the greatest obstacle to the Church of England's re-discovery of its true identity and function. This is an area of uncertainty which the Church of England shares with all the other English churches, and many other churches elsewhere, which have no links with the state and have for centuries enjoyed the freedom for which Miss Pitt craves. Admittedly, serious and searching questions need to be asked about the value and authenticity of the folk religion which so many Englishmen evidently still embrace, but it would be unwise in the extreme to dismiss this as being of little worth before the questions have been properly tackled, not least in an era in which the frontiers between faith and doubt, and between church and world, seem certain to become even less clearly defined than they are at present.

If disestablishment is ruled out, the choice is between the *status quo* and moderate reform. In the long term, the proposals of the Chadwick Report would benefit both church and state and ought, sooner or later, to be implemented. In the short term, it is not easy to see that, given the present attitudes, they would make much difference in practice. The question arises therefore as to the degree of priority which ought to be accorded to this particular issue. One of the points which rarely enters

into the church-state debate is the amount of time and
energy likely to be absorbed by the drafting and debating
of such legislation as would be required to bring any proposed changes into effect. The repeal of the 16th-century
Acts which govern the present arrangements would obviously be a matter for Parliament. But the Church of
England would then be required to produce a substantial
body of legislation – some of it of a controversial character – to replace the laws of the state. It is difficult to
believe that this would not be a highly complex and time-
consuming operation, and, after a period of more than
25 years in which the Church of England has done
precious little apart from attempting to re-order various
aspects of its own internal life, the prospect of spending
another lengthy spell in activity of a similar nature is
far from alluring – unless there are pressing practical
reasons for so doing.

There is also the ecumenical dimension to be taken
into account when discussing the urgency of change. Had
the Anglican-Methodist unity scheme been accepted, it
would obviously have been necessary to modify the
Church of England's relations with the state before Stage
2 of the scheme was reached and the two churches were
fully integrated. Unless the hope of reunion in England
was buried with the General Synod's 'No' to the
Methodists, it may be anticipated that a further round of
church unity talks – of a multilateral character – will
begin within the next decade and possibly reach a successful conclusion sometime in the 1980s. The Church of
England's state links are no longer a serious problem in
inter-church negotiations, but, as in the case of the
proposed union with the Methodists, the establishment
will have to go into the melting pot as soon as a new
united church begins to emerge. At the present juncture,
therefore, it would be a mistake for the Church of
England to become deeply involved in a matter which,
within the foreseeable future, will make very little difference to the ordering of its local life and which could
provide yet another distraction from the main task in the
parishes. This task requires it to sit very lightly on whatever privileges remain from the establishment, and to

co-operate on equal terms with all those other Christians who are seeking to serve God and their fellow men. Equally urgent is the need to offer a Christian critique of contemporary society and, in particular, to show the church's concern for the underprivileged members of it. Without waiting for the repeal of Acts of Parliament, church leaders can shed the trappings and pomp which go with a privileged position in society. In all these ways the Church of England is free to demonstrate where its faith is really centred and so prepare for the day when it will have a new relationship with the English people. There is no reason why this new relationship should be any less creative than that of the past, provided that the church sees its primary role as service of the human race – whether gathered in village, town, national or international communities – and not the protection of its own rights and privileges.

chapter 7
Trial by Synod

Although the voice of the layman has never been completely silenced, the Church of England has never been a 'lay church' in the sense that the great mass of those who make up its membership have been closely involved in its decision-making processes. For the greater part of English history the close relationship which has existed between the church and the nation as a whole has ensured that those responsible for the political development of the country have been influential in the affairs of the church. Kings, princes, prime ministers and parliamentarians have often exercised more influence than bishops and priests, thus preserving the Church of England from the overt clericalism which, for many centuries, has been one of the chief characteristics of the Church of Rome. But the lay voices have been those of an elite and lay influence has been confined to those who, by fair means or foul, have secured for themselves positions of power in the life of the nation. The ordinary 'man in the pew' has never had much say, either in the life of his local parish church or in the corridors of ecclesiastical power.

At the Reformation the Church of England firmly resisted the charms of independency. The doctrine of the priesthood of all believers received little encouragement from 16th-century monarchs and bishops, and the chief effect of the Reformation in England was to be seen in the substitution of an educated clerk for a sacerdotal priest. As a result, clerical control of the church continued more or less unchecked. It is true that in many places the local lord of the manor exercised very considerable influence over what the parson said and did, but, again, the lay influence was that of an elite; which is hardly surprising since the church was functioning in an elitist society. So elitist, in fact, that even the parochial clergy had a very small voice in the affairs of the church as a whole. The ancient Convocations of Canterbury and York were suppressed in the early part of the 18th century and when they were revived in 1852 their membership was in no way representative of the clergy. The Lower House of the Convocation of Canterbury had 54 members elected by the clergy and no fewer than 124 *ex officio* members. The Lower House at York which did not meet until 1861 had 49 elected and 39 *ex officio* members. In effect, the Church of England was ruled by its bishops, with the parochial clergy safeguarded against the worst excesses of episcopal authority by the 'parson's freehold'.

Soon after the revival of the Convocations it was suggested that the laity might conceivably have an interest in church government and be able to make some contribution to it. Hence the setting up, in 1886 and 1892, of houses of laymen to serve as advisory bodies to the two Convocations. This led to the formation in 1903 of the Representative Church Council, consisting of the Convocations and their Houses of Laymen, but the Council had only an advisory function and no executive or legislative powers.

During this period certain parishes set up parochial church councils to assist in the leadership of the local church but, unlike the annual Vestry meeting, these had no statutory authority, nor any power. The first serious attempt to involve the layman in the government of the Church of England came as a result of the 'Life and Liberty' movement which dominated the English church scene for a few years in the period immediately following the First World War and which led to the setting up of the National Assembly of the Church of England. This new body (Church Assembly) comprising the Upper and Lower Houses of the Convocations, together with a House of Laity, was given the right to pass measures which, if approved by Parliament, had statutory force. At the same time Parochial Church Councils were made compulsory and rolls of lay electors were compiled.

The laity had 'arrived' – even if their powers were some-what circumscribed.

Yet, to anyone who witnessed the Church Assembly in action during the 50 years of its life, it was a matter for astonishment that so vigorous a reforming move-ment had produced, as its sole achievement, so tedious and so ineffective an instrument of church government. 'Life and Liberty' attracted into its membership many of the most able and lively members of the Church of England of the time – and some of the most influential. F. A. Iremonger has described its first meeting, held in St. Martin-in-the-Fields Vicarage on 29 March 1917: 'As each member entered, it was noticed by the others that he (or she) counted for something in the life of the church. Later, when the names of Council members were published, few of the larger lay professions were found to be unrepresented on it.'[1] William Temple became chair-man and resigned from the important parish of St. James, Piccadilly in order to promote the aims of the movement all over the country. The secretary was Dick Sheppard, the most remarkable priest of the Church of England in the present century. Behind these two men were Henry Scott Holland, of St. Paul's; Cyril Garbett, later to become Archbishop of York; E. S. Woods, a future Bishop of Lich-field; the Headmaster of Rugby, the Master of Balliol, the Dean of Westminster, a Regius Professor of Divinity, the Principal of Cuddesdon and many other notable figures. Their enthusiasm knew no bounds. In a speech at a mass meeting held in Queen's Hall, London, William Temple set out the aims of 'Life and Liberty' – dis-establishment and self-government for the church – and concluded:

The day is come that burns like fire, for Christ has cast his fire on the earth. Come out from your safety and comfort; come out from your habits and conventions. Listen for the voice of the wind as it sweeps over the world and stand where you may be caught in its onward rush. Not now in ecclesiastical debate; not now in the careful defence of established positions won long ago in the service of God's

[1] *William Temple, Archbishop of Canterbury*, by F. A. Iremonger, p. 221, Oxford University Press, 1948.

Kingdom to be rendered; but in the establishment of justice between nation and nation, between capital and labour, between men and women. Here is your task. Will you perform it? Or will you stay as you are, to flicker out, a lamp that gives no light, unmourned and even unnoticed? So the Spirit calls. And shall we be deaf to that call? We cannot heed it loyally and effectively unless we have such power of control over our own action as may enable us to become a united and compact striking force, knowing our goal and agreed about the way to reach it.[2]

When due allowance has been made for the rhetoric, it must still be admitted that the Church Assembly and Electoral Rolls were a surprising consequence of such a campaign. Within a few years, Dick Sheppard's disillusionment was complete:

I am tired to death of all this tinkering at domestic machinery, the reform of the Prayer Book, the multiplication of the Episcopate, and these countless committees and committeemen who are over busy in making their own church more effective. Efficiency cannot coerce the Holy Ghost, nor can a National Assembly based on Parliamentary methods.[3]

Looking back on the events of the time, F. A. Iremonger, himself a prominent member of 'Life and Liberty', wrote that at the outset of the Church Assembly 'there was a sharp and fateful struggle between two groups . . . who differed widely in their conception of its policy and its purpose and may be called, roughly, the legalists and the moralists. The struggle was a brief one. The legalists – of whom Sir Lewis Dibdin, the trusted adviser of Randall Davidson, will be remembered as the leader – were soon in control; the voice of the Assembly is now the voice of the administrator, not of the prophet.'[4] The reformers had made a serious, yet exceedingly common, miscalculation of the changes necessary to a renewal of the Church of England's life. On what occasion in history – political or ecclesiastical – has an elected assembly, with administrative responsibilties, ever exercised a prophetic role? The structure of institutions and the nature of prophecy

[2] *ibid*, p. 232.
[3] *The Impatience of a Parson* by H. R. L. Sheppard, p. 198, Hodder & Stoughton.
[4] Iremonger, *op. cit.*, p. 281.

combine to make this an impossibility. For one thing, prophets are rarely elected. For another, administrators are called to preserve an institution in its 'given' form, not to destroy it or to change its basic constitution. If the leaders of 'Life and Liberty' wished to change the character of the Church of England, they would have been better employed in promoting an educational programme designed to offer deeper insights into the meaning of the Christian faith and the nature of the church. Only when a significant number of people have accepted change at this level, is it possible to secure radical change in the structure of the ecclesiastical institution.

On the other hand, the achievements of the 'Life and Liberty' movement should not be underestimated. For more than 1,000 years the Church of England had been dominated by a clerical and lay elite. The patterns of this dominance were firmly entrenched in the customs, traditions and laws of the institution – and in the minds of the majority of its members. Such patterns are not easily disturbed. Yet 'Life and Liberty' managed to disturb them to the extent of introducing into the church a machinery which, if not deserving of the description 'democratic', at least provided the opportunity for close consultation between bishops, clergy and laity over a wide range of subjects affecting the life of the Christian community. It may be noted in passing that, in spite of the reforming spirit of the Second Vatican Council, the Roman Catholic Church has still to evolve a pattern of collegiality distantly approaching that which began in England when Parliament passed the Enabling Act in 1919. The subsequent growth in understanding of the role of the laity in the church is not unrelated to the work of the 'Life and Liberty' pioneers and it would indeed have been remarkable had the Church of England found the best form of central government without a period of experiment involving mistakes.

Many of the difficulties experienced by the Church Assembly throughout its entire life, and still evident in the new General Synod, are attributable to two special characteristics of the Church of England. First, its comprehensiveness. Sheltering beneath the Anglican umbrella

there are people with differing views of the church. Some
are conscious of the church as a universal society which
embraces men and women of many different races, social
classes and cultures and, while encompassing the entire
life of certain communities, stands outside them with
its own hierarchical cultus and authority structure. Then
there are those who see the church as the embodiment of
the religious life of a nation, taking to itself many of the
cultural characteristics of the nation. Others tend to
think of the church in terms of a sect or a denomination
which is the equivalent of a voluntary society, existing
alongside many other human groups in a national or
local community. Each of these views of the church calls
for a different form of government. The universal view
is concerned for the autonomy of the church and expects
it to be governed by its bishops and clergy. The national
view looks for a close relationship between church and
state in all matters concerning organization. The denominational view demands autonomy and democracy.
When all three approaches are contained within one
church there are obvious problems for those who are
trying to evolve an appropriate form of government. The
Church Assembly was always dogged by the strong conviction of its bishops and priests – shared to some extent
by the laity – that they must retain complete control
over all matters related to doctrine and worship. Hence
the power of veto conceded to the bishops and the con-
fining of decisions on doctrine and worship to the clerical
Convocations. This was carried through to diocesan conferences, where the bishop, constituting a House on his
own, had the power of veto, and also to the parochial
church councils where the parish priest had complete
responsibility for the ordering of worship. Others in the
Church Assembly were particularly conscious of the
ancient links with the state and desired to do nothing
that would cut the church off from the life of the nation
as a whole. And then there were those – not many – who
wished to see the Church of England ordering its own life
by some form of democratic government akin to that of
the English Free Churches. In the event, the Church of
England adopted a quasi-parliamentary system which

satisfied no one and was soon recognized to be cumbersome and highly inefficient.

The second difficulty arose from the Church of England's deep suspicion of all forms of centralization. This
stems from the Reformation Settlement which was carefully contrived to ensure that the English church would
never again be vulnerable to anything approaching papal
control. Hence the series of checks and balances to be
found within the Church of England's organization, all of
which prevent the accumulation of too much power in
too few hands. Unfortunately, this has caused the growth
of an introverted parochialism. The parish sees itself
largely as a self-contained unit. It is with reluctance that
it becomes involved in the affairs of the deanery, and
scarcely recognizes that the diocese exists. The diocese
is busy organizing its own life and the fewer the communications it receives from Church House, Westminster,
the happier it becomes. In circumstances such as these
it is not surprising that the inauguration of the Church
Assembly was not universally welcomed. Many of the
clergy felt that the new body would constitute a threat
to their independence and that they were destined eventually to become salaried employees of a large ecclesiastical
corporation. Their minds were not set at ease by the
news of a postcard which arrived at the 'Life and Liberty'
office from a churchwarden (Lt.-Col. R.A. retd.) which
read, 'I understand that now the Enabling Bill is through
we can get rid of our parson. Please send full particulars
by return.'[5] Since the clergy provided the main channel
of communication between the Church Assembly, their
lack of enthusiasm and interest served to isolate the new
organ of government from its constituency from the
moment of its inception. Kenneth Thompson emphasizes
this point strongly in his well documented and highly
perceptive survey of the events which led to the birth
of the Church Assembly and its subsequent development:

The failure to enlist the clergy as the vital connecting link
in the chain of communication between the Assembly and
the parishes had serious consequences in preventing the

[5] Quoted by Iremonger, *ibid*, p. 275.

development of an informed and sympathetic support for the Assembly in the church at large. Studies of organization functioning stress the importance of the personal link in communication processes, which cannot be considered as simply a functional alternative to formal, written transmission of information.[6]

This lack of sympathetic support was quickly felt in the shortage of money available for the Assembly's use. A target of £5 millions had been fixed for a Central Church Fund but only £250,000 was raised. This left the Assembly dependent upon the contributions of the dioceses, who in turn had to extract the money from the parishes, and since the dioceses frequently failed to remit the amount expected of them the new instrument of government was always short of funds. Finance also provided a further point of tension between the clergy and the laity. Although distinguished bankers and stockbrokers might be prepared to concede that their knowledge of doctrinal and liturgical matters was less profound than that of bishops and deans, they were less ready to make concessions when financial matters were under discussion. Yet archbishops and bishops persisted in calling the tune, even though others were paying the piper and even providing him with his flute. Suggestions that the funds of the Ecclesiastical Commissioners (later to become the Church Commissioners) might become open to the influence of the Church Assembly, or even allocated in part to the Assembly, always aroused great controversy and some ill feeling, since the clergy felt that this money had been provided exclusively for their stipends and that any diversion to the general funds of the church could only mean that they were being required to subsidize projects and services which ought to be a charge on the whole church.

The Church of England's central government has, therefore, always been starved of the financial resources necessary to its functioning on a large scale, or even with a reasonable degree of efficiency, though it has been remarkably successful in attracting into its service a

6 *Bureaucracy and Church Reform* by Kenneth A. Thompson, p. 186, Oxford University Press, 1970.

succession of able laymen and priests who have made the best possible use of the resources available and received far more brickbats than bouquets for their pains. The staff at Church House is only one-third the size of that employed by the Church Commissioners and, until quite recently, was poorly paid – salary scales approximating to those of the voluntary church societies rather than to those of the civil service or equivalent administrative services. During the past fifty years the size of the organization has grown in an *ad hoc* fashion to meet new needs. Departments have been established to deal with special interests and responsibilities, and under the tidy influence of the late Archbishop Fisher four major boards were set up to rationalize the activities of the numerous small offices. Throughout this period of development, however, there has remained the constant problem of a parliamentary form of government lacking the machinery which parliaments have discovered to be necessary to their effective working. There is no 'government' to offer programmes or policies and to ensure their implementation; only a series of Commissions appointed to examine particular situations and more or less guaranteed before they begin that any proposals for change they feel moved to make will be treated with suspicion, if not with contempt. Equally serious, there is no 'cabinet' to give coherence and direction to policy-making. Between the meetings of the 'parliament' (three or four times a year) there is no one, apart from a Standing Committee with limited powers, in control of the situation. This weakness, and several others, were noted by a committee which reported to the Church Assembly in 1956 and concluded:

What is required at the centre to meet the needs of the present day is not an authoritarian bureaucracy, but an organization existing for the mutual advantage of the dioceses, adequately controlled, and sufficiently flexible to be capable of easy and rapid adjustment. Flexibility is achieved partly by effective control and partly by giving the subordinate bodies general directions rather than detailed terms of reference. In anything so large as the Assembly effective control can only be exercised through a body upon which the Assembly and its chief Councils are represented, which is able to give detailed consideration to, and to judge any proposal in the light of, the general needs and resources of the church. Finance is something integral with policy and cannot be dissociated from it.[7]

The formation of the four major departments was one of the results of this report, but the majority of its proposals were rejected on the grounds that they would introduce elements of bureaucracy into an organization where these were believed to be unnecessary and undesirable. An attempt to secure approval for the formation of something approaching a cabinet towards the end of the Church Assembly's life failed on similar grounds. The spectre of a curial form of government developing between Lambeth and Westminster was sufficient to unite the overwhelming majority of members in firm opposition.

The unsatisfactory basis of the Church Assembly became obvious for all to see when the process of revising the Church of England's Canon Law began in 1947. This was to keep the Convocations and the Church Assembly occupied for twenty years, and it must be accounted an utter disaster that many of the best minds in the church were turned in this, entirely irrelevant, direction during a crucial time of post-war development when English society was changing more dramatically than at any other period in history. Since the Canons involved matters of doctrine, worship and church order, they fell within the province of the Convocations. Yet, because they were binding upon the laity as well as upon the clergy, it was thought desirable that laymen should have some say in their new form. Thus it was arranged that after a Canon had been subjected to revision by the Convocations it should be sent to the House of Laity of the Church Assembly for comment. It was then returned to the Convocations for further consideration, and possibly further revision, in the light of the laity's suggestions. One hundred and twelve Canons underwent this treatment and when the process was completed in 1969

[7] *Report of the Committee on Central Funds*, Church Information Office, 1956.

members of the Church of England were made aware that a man might not marry his mother or his daughter, that the clergy should prepare for Confirmation any who desired to be Confirmed, that a copy of the Book of Common Prayer must be kept in every church and that the apparel of the clergy should be suitable to their office, save for purposes of recreation and other justifiable reasons. Thus illuminated, the church decided that the time had arrived to bring the Convocations and the House of Laity into closer relationship. A General Synod was proposed, but this ran into difficulties because it appeared to be – and in fact was – taking away most of the power of the Convocations. The Lower House of York was particularly resistant to this, partly because of a deep-rooted conservatism but also because it feared that the government of the church would become dominated by a London-based bureaucracy. In the end, and after a certain amount of horse-trading, it was agreed that the archbishops should appoint a Commission to produce a scheme for synodical government, but it was stressed that the fears of the Convocation of York must be taken into account when formulating proposals. Lord Hodson was appointed chairman of the Commission and had the assistance of four bishops, two canons, one professor, a baronet, a knight and five untitled laypeople. They reported in 1966.

Before considering their proposals, however, it is necessary to consider briefly the development of church government at other levels of the Church of England's life. The Enabling Act had prescribed Electoral Rolls and Parochial Church Councils as the base of the governmental pyramid. Considerable controversy (leading to the resignation of Charles Gore from the bishopric of Oxford) surrounded the discussions about the qualifications to be required of the new electors. Some thought Baptism sufficient, others believed Communicant status to be essential, but the former emerged victorious and, to the ringing of church bells, some $3\frac{1}{2}$ millions were enrolled. Not all of these – in fact, only a small proportion – wished to be involved in ordering the affairs of their local churches, and when it turned out that their primary task was the raising of money the number was reduced even further. Commenting on this in 1933, the editor of *Crockford's Clerical Directory* said: 'The whole scheme of rolls, councils, etc., was an attempt to create an interest rather than to meet a demand. The number of names on the roll has very little relation to the quality or vigour of the church life of the parish.' The rolls themselves were revised so infrequently that in certain parishes the majority of those whose names appeared on them were connected with the church only by reason of the fact that their bodies were interred in the church-yard. The consequences were serious for those who had hoped that the Enabling Act would bring life as well as liberty to the local churches. One bishop is reported as saying in the 1930s:

The annual meetings for the election of the parochial church councils are often almost farcical . . . This distressing un-reality at the basis of the autonomous system strikes an incapacitating weakness throughout the whole system.[8]

Twenty-five years later, the Archdeacon of Hastings, in an authoritative book on the organization of the Church of England, concluded, sadly:

It is evident that the ordinary member of the Church of England is not greatly interested in the democratic govern-ment of the church, and that his experience of it during the past twenty-five years has not aroused his enthusiasm. It follows that the claims of the councils of the church, from the Church Assembly to the parish, to be representative of lay opinion are not well founded.[9]

It must be recognized, however, that in some parishes – enough to be significant – the Parochial Church Councils did come to have an important role. Elections to them have never been strongly contested, except on occasions of local controversy, and their members are representative of the activists, rather than of the typical church attender, but this is common to practically all English institutions, including local government, and need occasion no great

[8] Quoted in *Crockford's Clerical Directory*, 1934.
[9] *The Church of England: Its members and its business* by Guy Mayfield, p. 59, Oxford University Press, 1958.

surprise. Where the parish priest has been prepared to see
the laity as an integral part of the church and partners
with him in its mission and ministry, the Parochial
Church Councils have played a prominent part in the
life of local churches and their responsibilities have
increased with the recent development of a 'theology of
the laity'. Unfortunately, the same cannot be said of the
Ruridecanal and Diocesan Conferences. Intended as a
meeting place for representatives from parishes in a particular neighbourhood, Ruridecanal Conferences had no
powers, although it was the custom in some dioceses for
them to be entrusted with the none too popular task of
allocating the amounts to be paid by parishes to diocesan
funds. Their half-yearly meetings were therefore given
over to listening to a speaker on some edifying, but rarely
exhilarating, topic, followed by two or three irrelevant
questions from those members of the Conference who
were still awake, and concluding with the blessing of a
grateful rural dean who was anxious to get home in
time for the 9 o'clock news on radio or television.
Parishes appointed representatives whose vocation was to
martyrdom rather than to mission. The Diocesan Conferences were hardly better, although their size and the
presence of the bishop and other diocesan worthies made
the gathering more of an 'occasion'. Designed as the
counterpart of the Church Assembly, the Diocesan Conference had no legislative function, apart from appointing
a board of finance to handle the relatively small amounts
of money available for expenditure in the diocese. It
received reports from the various boards and committees
of the diocese, and made appointments to them, but
exercised no executive responsibility. Indeed, it is difficult to see how these Conferences could ever have played
a significant part in government of any kind. In the more
enthusiastic dioceses they met twice a year – usually on
a weekday when only the clergy and laymen from the
professional or leisured classes could be present – but
in many places an annual meeting was deemed sufficient.
Membership consisted of all the diocesan clergy and
representatives from every parish, thus making for an
assembly of a thousand or more people. In those places

where the diocesan bishop had something to say, the presidential address might be worth listening to, but all too soon the platform was occupied by a speaker from afar, pleading a cause so remote from the lives of those present that any danger of action being demanded was automatically eliminated.

In these circumstances, the appointment of the Hodson Commission could scarcely be regarded as premature. It reported in 1966 and its proposals, largely unamended, came into effect with the inauguration of the General Synod by the Queen in November 1970. The most significant words in the Hodson Report – comforting for some, alarming for others – came in the opening sentence of its first proposal: 'We recommend that the General Synod should not be a new body, but a renamed and reconstituted Church Assembly in whom would be vested the functions and authority of the Convocations.'[10] Thus were the hopes dashed of those looking for a form of government that would avoid the fundamental problems encountered during the previous fifty years. The General Synod now has full legislative authority over all matters, including worship and doctrine, which concern the life of the Church of England. It has power to pass measures which are then submitted for approval by Parliament. It can make Canons and submit these for Royal Assent. Whereas the Church Assembly had 746 members, the General Synod has 545 and the number of *ex officio* members has been considerably reduced. Meetings are held three times a year, and sometimes they are held in the Province of York. The Synod is divided into three Houses: the House of Bishops consists of the 43 archbishops and diocesan bishops; the House of Clergy is made up of 251 priests, elected by or representing the diocesan and other clergy; the House of Laity has 251 members elected by the lay members of Deanery Synods or appointed by other groups. Generally, it is expected that the Synod will debate and vote together but, at the request of 25 members, the voting is by Houses and a motion must then receive a majority in all three

---

[10] *Government by Synod*, p. 68, Church Information Office, 1966.

Houses before it is deemed to be carried. This gives each House the power of veto. When matters related to doctrine and worship are under consideration, these must be submitted to the House of Bishops and can only be approved by the Synod in terms proposed by the bishops. If changes are proposed in services of Baptism, or Holy Communion or in the Ordinal, or if a scheme of union with another church is contemplated, these must be approved by a majority of the Diocesan Synods before the General Synod can pass the necessary Measures or Canons.

The only point of serious controversy in the Hodson proposals concerned the future of the Convocations of Canterbury and York. Mindful of the sensitivities of the clergy, it was recommended that the Convocations should remain in existence – their membership consisting of the bishops and the clergy elected to the General Synod – and be allowed to consider matters of doctrine and worship, when they so desired, before proposals for change were finally presented to the entire Synod. A similar right was extended to the House of Laity, but it was anticipated that such separate gatherings would be relatively infrequent. The Convocations were to be authorized to meet whenever they wished to discuss matters of particular concern to the clergy or their own Province of the church. To those who wished to see the Convocations retaining their old power, these proposals were far from satisfactory. Those who advocated the subsumption of the Convocations under the General Synod pointed out that, since virtually all the teeth of the Convocations were to be drawn, they could in the future be little more than a time-consuming clerical debating society. But political considerations demanded the retention of the Convocations, so they continue to exist, meet rarely, and exercise no significant influence over the Church of England's affairs.

In an effort to make synodical government effective at the local level, the Diocesan Conference has been replaced by a Diocesan Synod which has a membership of between 150 and 250. Its function is to concern itself with the affairs of the diocese and to consider and express an opinion 'on any other matters of religious or public interest'. It is also to advise the bishop on any matters which he may refer to it, to consider and express an opinion on matters referred to it by the General Synod and to keep the Deanery Synods informed about diocesan policies and problems. There are two Houses – clergy and laity – and the Diocesan Synod must meet at least twice a year. This hardly seems excessive in view of its suggested agenda. The Synod must also elect a Bishop's Council, whose function is to deal with any matters which the bishop chooses to refer to it rather than to the Synod as a whole. The power and influence of the bishop is still considerable. While he is under obligation to consult the Diocesan Synod on matters of general concern and importance to the diocese, there are obvious limits to the amount of business that can be transacted by a fairly sizeable assembly meeting twice or three times a year. Furthermore, the bishop has the power 'to withdraw from the Synod any matter falling within his pastoral office and inherent episcopal rights, for his own personal decision.'[11] What these matters and rights may be is not specified. Some are obvious – such as matters affecting the personal life and work of individuals – but the general vagueness of this provision seems out of place in a church attempting to be collegial and leaves a convenient door open for any bishop who may be addicted to prelacy.

The new Deanery Synods, replacing the useless Ruridecanal Conferences, are intended to provide a further tier of government between the diocese and its parishes. In common with their higher authorities, these are to consider and express an opinion on any subject that takes their fancy, especially if it relates to the affairs of the Church of England. They are also to foster common policies on the problems of the area, implement any decisions of the Diocesan Synod, consider matters referred to them by the Diocesan Synod, refer matters up to the diocese and also elect the members of the Diocesan Synod. Again, there are Houses of clergy and laity – the former

[11] *Government by Synod*, p. 47.

consisting of all the clergy of the Deanery and the latter elected by Parochial Church Councils. The rural dean and an elected member are joint chairmen. Total membership ranges from 50-100 and meetings are held three or four times a year. The Parochial Church Councils have not been affected by the new synodical arrangements, but they are now required to revise their Electoral Rolls every year and to prepare entirely new rolls every sixth year.

On paper, the arrival of synodical government constituted a major reform in the life of the Church of England and the culmination of a process which began with the Enabling Act of 1919. It was an important part of the programme of renewal advocated by the Parish and People Movement in the 1960s. The elections for the new General Synod were contested with unusual vigour in 1970. Anglo-catholics and Evangelicals offered opposition to the Anglican-Methodist unity scheme as a key point in their manifestoes and at the same time assured the clergy that they were against anything akin to the Morley Report proposals on deployment and payment. A body calling itself the New Synod Group was sponsored by Parish and People and employed a full-time secretary to encourage and support candidates who were committed to reform and renewal in certain areas of the church's life. More than 200 of those elected had had no previous experience of church government in the old Church Assembly. The use of proportional representation had made the elections a highly complex operation (in the diocese of London there were more than 50 candidates for 13 clergy seats), but when the results were announced one church paper commented:

On the whole it appears that the election has produced a synod which will reflect pretty accurately the present make-up of the Church of England – i.e. roughly 25 per cent Radical/Reformist, 25 per cent Evangelical, 10 per cent Anglo-catholic, 40 per cent mixture of Everything and Nothing. From such a body it would be reasonable to expect a modicum of reform but obviously nothing resembling a revolution.[12]

[12] *The Christian Century*, 4 November, 1970.

Subsequent events were soon to demonstrate the accuracy of this assessment. After the panoply of the Royal inauguration was over, the Synod got down to business and soon one member new to central church government was constrained to complain that the proceedings were being dominated by the 'old hands' of the Church Assembly. This was not altogether surprising in the early stages for the 'new boys' had to learn the procedural ropes and become acclimatized to their surroundings. Yet, two years later it is painfully obvious that the Hodson Commission's first recommendation has been carried out most faithfully: the General Synod is not a new body; it is the old Church Assembly reconstituted and renamed. The style and atmosphere of the Synod is indistinguishable from its predecessor. Those who entered with the intention of shaking the Church of England to its foundations have now discovered that the machinery of ecclesiastical government is not easily moved and that the Synod is able to absorb and neutralize the most savage of assaults upon the *status quo*. Not that savage assaults are very frequent or indeed an effective way of securing attention. As in the case of the House of Commons, it is of the greatest importance that a speaker should 'catch' the distinctive atmosphere of the place, otherwise he will not be heard, be his points never so true or so relevant to the subject under discussion. He should exhibit those civilized attributes which are the hallmark of attendance at a 'good school' – loyalty to the institution, gentle humour and subtle irony, unfailing courtesy and no hint of personal denigration, due respect for those of higher status, social or ecclesiastical, and no trace of awkwardness or abrasiveness. Thus are movements towards violent change effectively neutralized.

At the lower (many Anglicans will contest this adjective) levels, the story is much the same. The Diocesan Synods, though smaller than the old Conferences, are remarkably similar to them in composition and atmosphere. Some bishops are eager to share their ideas, policies and problems with a representative gathering of this kind and, in these circumstances, purposeful meetings are held. Others, seemingly without ideas, policies or problems,

E

find it difficult to co-operate with a Synod and resort to the well-tested and frustrating standby of a 'visiting speaker'. But, given the best will and imagination in the world, the Diocesan Synods are severely limited in their scope. Their size, infrequency of meeting and, above all, their lack of power, means that they can be little more than consultative or deliberative assemblies. As such they may perform a valuable function, but the function is not that of government. Reports from Deanery Synods indicate a similar problem. Where the leadership is strong and resourceful, these Synods can perform a useful function in bringing together representatives of local churches in a particular area to consider common opportunities and problems, and to encourage co-operation between parishes. But their powers are extremely limited. They must rely almost entirely on good leadership and a generous spirit of co-operation. Where these are lacking, action is virtually impossible and the most able representatives become disillusioned. There is no evidence to suggest that Parochial Church Councils are any better informed than they were previously about matters under consideration at Deanery, Diocesan and General Synod levels, so the fatal weakness of the pre-synodical days remains.

It is far from easy to see how the Church of England can evolve a more effective form of government without major changes in its convictions about its own nature and role. Certain minor improvements will be made to the new synodical system in the light of experience of its operation. Weekend meetings, firmly resisted by the Hodson Commission but now being introduced on an occasional basis, may lead to the election of a different kind of layman in 1975. The communications problem is not intractable and ought to be tackled as a matter of urgency, though the best methods will be ineffective if the activities of the General and Diocesan Synods do not appear to be related to the issues which are conceived as important in the parishes. The Diocesan Synods will either have to meet more frequently or be spared some of the documents remitted to them by the General Synod, in order that they may fulfil their primary role, which is concern for the work of the church in the diocese.

But when all these things have been achieved, the fundamental problem will remain. It was accurately summar-
ized by Kenneth Thompson at the end of his sociological
survey of the government of the Church of England
during the period 1800-1965:

The basic dilemma which had faced the Church of England
in its organisational response to social change had been to
adjust itself to the process of differentiation of institutional
domains, whilst at the same time maintaining its basic
identity as a coalition of diverse principles of authority and
doctrine.[13]

Any suggestion that equal representation of clergy and
laity in the General Synod is a negation of the democratic
process, when the church has more than $2\frac{1}{2}$ million lay
electors but only 18,000 clergymen, is certain to be rejected because of the theological view of the place of the
clergy held by the majority of Anglicans. Similarly, if
it is suggested that the powers of any of the three Houses
in the General Synod ought to be curtailed, so that
legislation cannot be blocked by bishops, clergy or laity
acting in isolation, questions arise as to the role of these
groups in the Christian community. Moves in the direction of further centralization and the setting up of a
'cabinet' raise other issues about the nature of the church
and the relationship between the local, the national and
the universal. Anyone advocating a more overtly political
approach to church government, with organized parties,
policy statements, the deliberate seeking of power and
the systematic pursuit of specific objectives will soon be
confronted with the fact that the Church of England does
not conceive itself as remotely resembling any secular
institution in which such an approach would be acceptable and, indeed, eminently desirable. Hints that the
income of the Church Commissioners ought to be placed
at the disposal of the General Synod will inevitably cause
the clergy to rebel because they believe that such a move
would threaten their independence and jeopardize their
prophetic role. Anything designed to administer the
church as if it were similar to other voluntary bodies

[13] Kenneth A. Thompson, *op. cit.*, p. 237.

provokes endless argument and sharp division of opinion about the proper relationship between the community of faith and the secular world.

There is no prospect of the Church of England reaching a common mind on any of these issues within the foreseeable future, so it is pointless to think in terms of alternative forms of government which are significantly different from that which has been recently established. This can only mean a continuation of the slow, ponderous and largely ineffective government which has characterized the past 50 years. In these circumstances it is important that local churches should retain as much freedom for manoeuvre as is consonant with membership of the one, holy, catholic and apostolic church of Christ. The fact that the church's central organs of administration are unable to move quickly must not be allowed to prevent parishes and larger units from responding to the changes and challenges of the societies in which they are called to minister. It is therefore necessary for the General Synod to recognize its limitations and, while striving to perfect its own life, to facilitate the freedom of the local churches and encourage them to exploit this freedom to the full.

chapter 8

Treasure on Earth

Many of the problems facing the Church of England are complex and cannot be quantified. Not so its financial position, which lends itself to precise analysis of past and present and reasonably confident forecasts of the future. Here is one area of the church's life where it is possible to locate very high levels of efficiency and expertise. The day is long past when *The Times* could ask:

What has the Ecclesiastical Commission done since 1836? It has received and expended a great deal of money. Unhappily, it appears that the expenditure has been greater than the receipts. This is not surprising when we learn how its funds have been regulated. Balance, audit, account, were for nine years, it seems, words unknown to the Commission. In any case, the things they represent were wanting. The sole record of its pecuniary transactions were to be found in the mangled remains of the Secretary's cheque-book.[1]

It is unfortunate, therefore, that today's efficiency and expertise cannot produce a happier story, though it will soon become apparent that without these qualities there would be no story to tell. The blunt truth is that if the Church of England is to maintain its organizational life on the present scale it will, during the next 3-4 years, have to persuade its members to increase their annual contributions by at least 50 per cent. Never before has it faced such a serious financial crisis, the magnitude of which was outlined in the summer of 1972 by a small group appointed by the Archbishops of Canterbury and York to keep the Church of England's needs and resources under constant review. Their report said:

If we project the church's financial needs in 1970 forward

---

[1] *The Times*, 7 February 1850, quoted by Kenneth A. Thompson, *op. cit.*, p. 65.

to 1975, estimating on the basis of known inflation in 1971 and thereafter at the rate of 5 per cent as in our earlier reports, the needs of 1975 will be £77 million. The Church Commissioners would hope to be able to provide nearly £32 million, leaving a balance of some £45 million to be met. The laity gave a total of some £31 million in 1970, so that the needs of the church, if its existing structure is to be maintained, will in 1975 present a challenge to church members to find an additional £14 million. In effect this means every church member giving nearly half as much again as he gave in 1970. But costs in the next few years might well rise faster than in the period of 1963–68 and the rate of inflation from now until 1975 might conceivably go as high as in the beginning of 1971, say 10 per cent per annum or even more; or it might be somewhere between the two. In that case the challenge to the church would be even greater and the laity would need to do more than give half as much again as they did before. It might be necessary for them to find anything up to twice as much as they did in 1970.[2]

Just over half the expenditure of the Church of England goes on the maintenance of its full-time servants – mainly the clergy – while the rest is devoted to the maintenance of church buildings and services, education, capital projects and central and diocesan services. The actual figures for 1970 and the projected figures for 1975 are as follows:

	1970	1975
	£ millions	
1. The Maintenance of the Ministry (including deaconesses and lay workers)		
(a) Stipends	20.4	27.5
(b) Working Expenses	1.1	3.9
(c) House Maintenance	2.9	3.5
(d) Pensions	3.4	6.1
(e) Training	.5	.7
Sub-total	28.3	41.7
2. The maintenance of worship of the church	11.9	16.0
3. Education	2.3	3.1
4. Capital needs	10.0	12.4
5. Central and diocesan services	2.9	3.8
	55.4	77.0

The total expenditure in 1968 was £50.5 millions

[2] *The Church's Needs and Resources: A Sixth Report*, p. 9, Church Information Office, 1972.

As the Archbishops' Advisers make clear, these increases are not due to any expansion of the church's work. They are simply the result of inflation. In order to calculate their figures for 1975, the Advisers have taken account of clergy manpower trends (a decline of 1,500 in the number of those in full-time employment is anticipated) and assumed increased costs at the rate of 5 per cent per annum between 1972 and 1975. Unless the inflationary spiral in Britain is brought under firm and rapid control, this seems certain to be a conservative estimate and price increases in the range of 5-10 per cent would make a considerable difference to the figures quoted above. In an inflationary situation it may of course be anticipated that the wages and salaries of church members will rise, and that they will therefore be able to increase their contributions to meet additional costs, but it remains for the church to convince its members of the need for higher levels of giving and this is far from easy in a church where, until comparatively recently, the laity have not been required to provide much financial support.

In May 1970, the Archbishops' Advisers recommended that the Incumbent of a parish should not receive an annual income below the range of £1,500-£1,700, except in special circumstances. Without wishing to compare a clergyman's work and needs with any other profession, they kept in mind the level of salaries enjoyed by teachers and social workers. In addition to his stipend an Incumbent receives a free house (rates and repairs paid) and shares in a non-contributory pension scheme. It is not easy to calculate the value of these benefits but the Advisers suggested that an average of about £900 a year would be reasonable. They were, therefore, thinking in terms of an equivalent of £2,500 a year, though it has to be remembered that some parsonage houses are both expensive and uncomfortable and that a tied house is neither a personal asset nor a place of refuge in retirement. By July 1971, the Advisers were pointing out that in order to maintain the value of their 1970 recommendations the income range would have to be raised to £1,650-£1,870. At the end of 1970 the Central Register of Benefice Income[3] showed that the income of Incumbents fell into the following groups—

Range of Income	No. of Incumbents	Percentage
Under £1,100	140	1½
£1,100 to £1,199	552	5¾
£1,200 to £1,299	1,559	16½
£1,300 to £1,399	2,135	22½
£1,400 to £1,499	1,794	19
Total under £1,500	6,180	65¼
£1,500 to £1,599	1,155	12¼
£1,600 to £1,699	729	7¾
£1,700 to £1,799	441	4¾
£1,800 to £1,899	299	3
£1,900 to £1,999	184	2
	8,988	95
£2,000 and over	483	5
	9,471	100

Thus two-thirds of Incumbents were below £1,500 – the lower end of the recommended range – and by the end of 1971 49 per cent were still below this figure. The recommended range for assistant curates is £930 a year rising to £1,170 after seven years, while Deaconesses and Licensed Women Workers move from £775 to a maximum of £1,165, but these are recommended stipends and, as in the case of Incumbents, not every assistant curate, Deaconess and Woman Worker receives his or her due. Neither does every Incumbent receive reimbursement of the expenses he incurs in the course of performing his duties. These include such items as postage, stationery, telephone, car running expenses and depreciation, secretarial assistance, office equipment and robes. During the year ending 31st March 1968 they amounted to an average of £213 per Incumbent, but the amounts reimbursed by their parishes averaged only £63. It is now estimated that during 1971 Incumbents were, in effect, subsidizing

[3] *Church Commissioners for England: report and accounts 1971.*

their parish budgets to the tune of £200. The responsibility for ending a situation which would not be tolerated in any other profession for one minute has been laid at the doors of Parochial Church Councils but many parishes, especially in artisan areas, are either unwilling or unable to meet their obligations. The total shortfall on clergy stipends and expenses in 1970 was of the order of £4½ million, but the Archbishops' Advisers warn that it could be as high as £13 million in 1975 if inflation were 10 per cent per annum.

An analysis of the £11.9 million spent on the maintenance of the worship of the church in 1970 shows that £3 million was paid to organists, vergers and other employees; the maintenance of church buildings, heating, lighting, insurance and equipment cost £7.4 million, and £1.5 million was devoted to the maintenance of halls and other buildings. All these items are obviously vulnerable to inflationary trends and the estimated figure of £16 million for 1975 is hardly excessive. Expenditure on education can be divided into two categories. Sunday School, youth work and university chaplaincies absorb relatively modest amounts of money, but church schools and colleges of education require astronomical sums. The Archbishops' Advisers believe that an outlay of between £13 million and £18 million will be required on church schools alone during the next 15 years if the church is to meet its present commitments. Not surprisingly, they say that this is in the realm of the impossible and unless some other major source of income can be found the financing of church schools will break down. Capital needs in the parishes, which now absorb £10 million a year, include the modernization or replacement of unsuitable clergy houses, the erection of churches and clergy houses in new housing areas, and extraordinary repairs to churches, halls and organs. It is anticipated that expenditure on new churches will not rise very much and may actually decrease a little, but it must be assumed that the cost of major repairs to ageing church buildings will continue to rise. All in all, the total cost of keeping the church's buildings going is about £17 million a year.

In any consideration of the Church of England's

buildings, and the cost of their repair and maintenance, it is necessary to distinguish between various categories of building. There are the cathedrals, most of which are not only mother churches of dioceses but also architectural treasures of major importance to the English nation. Of lesser importance, but still an integral part of the country's cultural heritage, are the ancient parish churches, a few of which are no longer needed by the church but the overwhelming majority of which are still in regular use. Then come the churches built during the past 150 years, mainly in the late-Victorian era, which for the most part have little architectural merit and all too often present major problems because of their size and location. The more recent buildings obviously raise questions about the cost of their erection and use, rather than their maintenance and repair, though it will not be surprising if the church's post-war building programme begins to present major maintenance problems before the present century is out.

Turning first to the cathedrals, it is clear that buildings of their age and size will always be a financial problem. Since the end of the Second World War, nearly all of them have been the subject of major appeals – often to make good the ravages of a long period of neglect – and it is reasonable to suppose that the raising of money will never be far from the minds of their Deans and Chapters. The direct cost to the Church of England of restoration programmes is, however, relatively small. Because the cathedrals are national monuments, and frequently the most significant piece of architecture in a county or region, they can draw financial support from a much wider field than that occupied by those who share actively in the church's life. A report sent to members of cathedral chapters in 1969 by the fund-raising firm of Hooker Craigmyle and Company demonstrated this most clearly. The firm was at that time directing appeals for the cathedrals at Winchester (target £405,000), Salisbury (target £250,000) and York (target £2 million) and they stated quite frankly that, in their experience, raising money for diocesan needs, such as new churches and pastoral work, was a great deal more difficult than fund

raising for historic cathedrals. With their three appeals
well on the way to reaching the targets, it was possible
for the report to indicate where the money was actually
coming from and the average of the sources was as follows:

Category of Donor	Percentage at 1 April, 1968
Industry (inside diocese)	9.2
Industry (outside diocese)	12.7
Individuals (inside diocese)	22.4
Individuals (outside diocese)	7.9
Local authorities	16.1
Parochial Church Councils	2.2
Trusts and Foundations	13.6
Overseas Gifts	.6
Special events	1.8
Friends – corporate gifts	7.5
Other bodies (schools, hospitals etc).	2.9
Legacies, boxes, etc.	1.1

It will be seen from these figures that the direct contribution of the Church of England was comparatively insignificant. The Church Commissioners gave token dona-
tions – £2,000 to Winchester, £2,500 to Salisbury and
£15,000 to York – while the parishes of the three dioceses
actually gave less than schools, hospitals and other voluntary societies. No doubt there were churchpeople among
the individuals who provided just over one-fifth of the
money from within the dioceses. Here there were significant differences between York and the two southern
cathedrals. Owing to the magnitude of York's need and
to the special claim which the Minster is able to make
upon the powerful loyalties of the inhabitants of England's largest county, it proved relatively easy to obtain
substantial contributions from industry and local authorities. By 1 April, 1968 no less than 69 per cent of the £1½
million then raised had come from these two sources.
Individual contributions for York amounted to only 16.2
per cent of the total, compared with 31.8 per cent at
Winchester and 43 per cent at Salisbury. The current
appeal for St. Paul's Cathedral is proving to be spectacu-
larly successful. Launched in February 1971 with a
target of £3 million, the appeal fund had reached £2.35
million in sixteen months, no less than £170,000 having

come from the United States. Again, the direct cost to the Diocese of London was minimal and, with the cathedrals attracting more visitors than at any other time in their history, it is now generally recognized that these lovely buildings are a national responsibility.

It should not be supposed from this, however, that the Church of England is not affected by these major appeals for cathedrals. There is no way of assessing how much of the money given by individuals and corporate bodies might otherwise have found its way into local church projects. In the light of Hooker Craigmyle's experience, perhaps very little. Yet when the Teesside Industrial Mission approached certain Yorkshire companies for a modest contribution to the support of their extremely important work, the most common response was: 'We are sorry to refuse you, but we have recently contributed a substantial sum to the York Minster appeal.' Another factor concerns appointments to cathedral deaneries. Since the cathedrals have a long history as centres of learning, it has been customary for their Deans to be men of learning, and some of the Church of England's greatest scholars have worked beneath the shadow of a cathedral tower. Here it should be noted that, although the influence of the church now predominates in the selection of bishops, the Crown retains a lively interest in the choice of deans and there is no guarantee that the man appointed to the leading post in a cathedral would be the first choice of either the bishop or the diocese. When financial matters loom so large in cathedral life, it would not be surprising if ability to raise money were rated higher than scholarship or even ideas when the list of candidates for deaneries is under scrutiny, and there is some evidence from recent appointments that this is in fact the case. If, for instance, the choice is between a clubbable man, who is an excellent after-dinner speaker and can be guaranteed to get on well with the business tycoons of the city or the landed gentry of the county, and a shy scholar who normally thinks twice, or even three times, before he utters and is more at home at a college high table than in a board room, and a controversial priest of left-wing views, who has been known to take part in demonstrations championing the cause of the underprivileged, it might well be that the deanery would go, not to the man who might have turned the cathedral into a great centre of Christian witness but to the man who would have little difficulty in raising half a million pounds for the restoration of its fabric.

No reliable figures are available for the cost to the Church of England of repairing and restoring the ancient parish churches. More than 8,000 of these were built before the Reformation and 11,000 are said to be sufficiently important from the architectural point of view to merit support from the Historic Churches Preservation Trust if need arose and funds were available.[4] This Trust, which raises money, mainly by subscriptions, to assist parishes which are unable to meet repair bills on their own, oversees the distribution of about £100,000 per annum for this purpose, but says that it could use four or five times this amount. Since 1952 it has raised £2 million and given grants to 2,500 churches. Anyone who has been responsible for the care of a mediaeval church is aware that in any ten-year period it is necessary to spend something in the region of £10,000 to maintain the building in good order. The compulsory quinquennial inspections are now preventing long periods of neglect, but it is one thing for an architect to say what needs to be done and quite another for the necessary funds to be raised. Quite often, the essential and urgent work is carried out, with the remainder left to an indefinite future. Even this can require much self-sacrifice from those who attend an ancient church and, in addition to contributing money from their own pockets, are called upon to devote time and imagination to extracting money from the pockets of other members of the local community. If attention is concentrated on the mediaeval buildings and it is estimated that approximately £1,000 will be required for each of them for each of the next ten years, the total bill facing the Church of England will be of the order of £80 million. Some of these buildings are now redundant and when they are conveniently situated

4 See interview with Canon Ian Dunlop, a member of the Trust, in the *Church Times*, 21 April, 1972.

may be turned to other uses and cease to be the church's responsibility. In the city of York, sixteen mediaeval churches serve a population of only 5,000 and it was proposed in 1967 that some of these should be used as concert halls, old people's day centres, museums or columbarium.[5] Similar proposals were made in 1970 for the city of Norwich, the inner area of which has 23 parish churches, some of which have already been closed or converted to other uses, serving a population of 4,000. More than half the income of the churches in Norwich is devoted to the repair and upkeep of buildings.[6]

Although the Victorians were slow off the mark with their church building programme and allowed huge populations to develop in the fast-growing towns and cities before dividing the ancient parishes, they built furiously once the spirit moved them. But hardly had their enormous churches been consecrated when the habits of worship began to change and people of a church-going disposition began to move away from town centres to the more comfortable suburbs. It is therefore hardly an exaggeration to say that the great majority of the Victorian town churches have been serious problems – liturgically as well as financially – for almost the whole of their lives. Just how serious a problem they have become to the Church of England was revealed in a survey carried out in the South London deanery of Battersea in 1966. The population of the area at that time was just over 110,000 and there were 16 Church of England parishes, each with its complex of church building, vicarage and hall or school. Until 1827 there was only one parish serving a quite small population of market gardeners, but during the next 80 years 15 new parishes were created to deal with a phenomenal increase in population due to the arrival of a railway terminus and many factories. Between 1861 and 1901 the population grew from 20,000 to 169,000, but it is now anticipated by the planning authorities that the future popula-tion of Battersea will be about 85,000. The total seating

[5] *New Uses for Old Churches*: the report of the York Redundant Churches Commission.
[6] *Norwich City Commission Report*, p.13.

in the 16 parish churches was 7,700. Average attendance at the main Sunday service in 1964 *in all the churches* was 942. This rose to about 1,700 at Christmas and Easter, and the total number on the parish electoral rolls was 2,751. Half the parishes were running at an annual financial loss and it was estimated that £97,550 was needed for capital expenditure on the buildings. Since 1966 two of the churches have been destroyed by fire, another has been pulled down to make way for a block of flats (though it is planned to use some of the proceeds to build a new church, hall and vicarage nearby), and three parishes have either been merged or are in process of merging. But obviously the provision of buildings remains wildly in excess of any foreseeable need and the drain on the church's resources continues unabated.

Under the 1968 Pastoral Measure problem buildings can be declared redundant, but the procedure is somewhat complicated and, although it has been estimated that over 2,000 church buildings in England are actually redundant, only a handful have been converted to other uses or demolished. During 1970 the Advisory Board for Redundant Churches considered 80 cases. It agreed to the demolition of 27, offered preliminary advice on the future of 35 and refused demolition certificates for the rest. The Board, which was set up in 1968 by the Archbishops of Canterbury and York to advise on the architectural and historical qualities of redundant churches, consists of seven specialists in the fields of architectural history, planning and conservation. It administers £80,000 a year on the preservation of buildings which, although redundant from the church's point of view, are deemed to be of architectural or historical importance. Half the money is provided by the state, half comes from the proceeds of the sale of redundant church sites following demolition. When a building is believed to be redundant, the local situation must be thoroughly investigated by the Diocesan Pastoral Committee. Needless to say, the initiation of such investigations normally causes a great outcry from the local inhabitants, the overwhelming majority of whom rarely set foot in the building concerned and contribute nothing to its maintenance. But if it is confirmed that the church is redundant, ownership is immediately transferred to the diocese, the parish is no longer responsible for its upkeep and services cease. Efforts must then be made to find an alternative use for the building and the search must not be abandoned until at least 12 months have elapsed. At this point the Advisory Board for Redundant Churches enters the picture. If the building is of outstanding architectural or historical importance, and no alternative use can be found for it, the Board may assume responsibility for its future. But the chairman, Lord Fletcher of Islington, stated in June 1971 that the £80,000 a year allocated for the purpose was 'wholly inadequate' and, with more than 700 buildings already in the pipeline, he hardly appeared to be exaggerating. Lord Fletcher also said, at a press conference to mark the publication of the Board's report for 1970, that the experience of two years had shown that the part of the Pastoral Measure, which established the Advisory Board and the Redundant Churches Fund, was by itself inadequate to deal with the problem of redundant churches, many of which are already in a very poor state of repair before they reach the stage of being declared redundant. If a building cannot be preserved, either because it is not regarded as important or because funds are not available, it may then be demolished. In some instances the sites realize large sums of money, but these are uncommon since redundant churches rarely occupy prominent city centre sites. The Norwich City Commission Report estimated that in half the cases where churches were proposed for demolition the site value would not greatly exceed the cost of demolition and the removal of monuments, etc. The chief financial benefit to the church would be the ending of the obligation to keep the buildings in repair.

It is now clear that the disposal of redundant buildings will provide the Church of England with one of its most severe headaches during the 1970s. Financial pressure, continuing decline in church attendance, social and personal mobility, and a greater desire that the church's resources should be used to the best advantage will combine to create a situation which will be well beyond the capacity of the present machinery to handle. The proper disposal of more than 2,000 buildings which house so much aesthetic, historical and emotional capital, can never be an easy undertaking, even when the procedures are sensitive and efficient. Yet the Church of England cannot be expected to survive – much less move forward – while this heavy millstone hangs from its neck.

The smallest item of expenditure listed on page 136 is devoted to the training of clergy and other full time workers. In comparison with the rest of the budget, the figure of £.5 million, rising to £.7 million, is relatively insignificant. But the financial problems associated with this figure seem certain to change the entire structure of theological education in the Church of England. When the 'boom years' of recruitment from 1959–63 were over, the principals and governing bodies of the twenty-one theological colleges found themselves short not only of students but also of cash. Institutions responsible for training an average of 50 students find it virtually impossible to finance more than two or three empty rooms, and the steeply rising costs of recent years have exacerbated this basic problem. The report of a Working Party set up under the Chairmanship of Sir Bernard de Bunsen indicated in 1968 that while the cost per student in colleges with more than 70 members had risen by only £2, from £356.9 per annum, to £358.7 per annum, during the four years 1963–66, the cost in colleges with under 50 members had risen by £49, from £369.8 to £418.8.[7] These figures presume that colleges are full to capacity, but by the end of 1967 only 1,060 of the available 1,369 places were occupied and four colleges were less than half full. In October 1970, following the closure of three colleges, the number of places had been reduced to 1,181, but by this time the number of students was only 834 and it was accepted by the Church Assembly during the early part of the same year that provision should be made for a maximum of 850 places during the next decade. All the colleges now find it necessary to

[7] *Theological Colleges for Tomorrow*, p. 59, Church Information Office, 1968.

draw increasingly on support from central church funds for both capital expenditure and ordinary running costs. And, since these funds are already under heavy pressure, financial considerations as well as educational needs are driving the Church of England very painfully to rationalize its theological education resources by grouping colleges together to form larger units.

Having examined the main outlets for the Church of England's expenditure, it is now necessary to turn to its sources of income. Here a division must be made between the 44 per cent of income provided by the Church Commissioners and the remainder which comes mainly from the voluntary contributions of church members. Turning first to the voluntary contributions and other local sources of income, these may be categorized as follows for the year 1970:[8]

	£ million
Stewardship and other regular giving	6.4
Covenanted subscriptions (gross)	5.8
Church cash collections and boxes	6.0
Gift Days, bazaars, fetes, etc.	2.7
Other miscellaneous gifts	2.1
Bank interest, dividends and fees	1.7
Income from church halls	1.5
Rents from property and income from trusts	.9
Special appeals for capital objects	5.8
Legacies and bequests	1.0
	33.9

It will be seen from these figures that well over one-third of local revenue comes from commitments to regular giving by individuals. Here it is possible to trace a spectacular rise in income during the period 1956–1968. In 1956 regular giving amounted to £2.5 million which represented 14.9 per cent of total parish income. By 1968 this had risen to £11.6 million, representing 38.0 per cent of income. The 1970 figures show a slight fall to 36 per cent of income. These figures are attributable to the growth of the Christian Stewardship movement which

[8] *The Church's Needs and Resources: 6th Report*, Appendix table 4.

reached England from the United States in the late 1950s
and encourages church members to commit themselves
to the giving of a regular amount of money every week,
instead of casual contributions on a collection plate. In
1956 some 752,000 people were known to belong to
planned giving schemes and their number had increased
to 1,018,000 by 1968. During the same period the amount
contributed under these schemes rose from 6½p per head
per week to 22p per head per week, and a further increase
to 29p was recorded in 1970. In assessing the amounts
given, account must of course be taken of the fall in the
value of money owing to inflation, but a report published
by the Church of England's Central Board of Finance in
1970 concluded that 'in general terms the amount of
giving to the church, and its financial resources, approximately kept pace with the increase in the amount of
money at the disposal of the people.'[9] Relating this to the
rise in costs to the church, the same report said, 'The
resources placed at the disposal of the church during
this time substantially exceeded anything necessary to
compensate for the rise in the cost of goods and services.' That this should have happened during a time
when church attendances have been declining is evidence
of the success of the Christian Stewardship movement
and also suggests that the church's membership may have
strengthened its general commitment. In view of the
warnings given by the Archbishops' Advisers, this commitment will have to be expressed even more clearly in
financial terms during the next five years and it remains
true that members of the Church of England contribute
far less to the support of their church than members of
any other Christian body in the country.

There can be no doubting that this low level of financial
support is due to the Church of England's ancient endowments which, over the centuries, have provided the
parishes with the services of one or more priests at little
or no direct local cost. Whereas the members of other
churches have been obliged to raise money (usually a
substantial proportion of the total budget of a local

[9] *The Christian Stewardship of Money*, p. 18, Church Information
Office, 1970.

church) to pay the stipend and housing of a priest or minister, Anglicans have enjoyed the luxury of a ministry whose income was derived from endowments or glebe. During the 19th and early part of the 20th centuries there was often an additional bonus in the form of a vicar who had a private income and paid many of the normal running expenses of the church out of his own pocket. Hence the present tardiness of some parishes in meeting the working expenses of their clergy and the marked lack of enthusiasm for raising money to pay the stipend of a priest. It is not necessary to trace the origins of the Church of England's endowments, most of which began with the allocation of certain pieces of land to provide an income (or at least a supply of food) for the priest of a particular parish. But no discussion of the Church of England's finances can ignore the existence of the Church Commissioners for England who provide nearly one half of the annual income and without whose activities the shape of the church would clearly be very different from anything observable today.

The beginnings of the Church Commissioners were modest enough, and the first Secretary who felt in the 1830s that 'the mangled remains of a cheque book' provided an adequate accounting system would doubtless be a little surprised to learn that at 31 March, 1971 the assets of the Commissioners totalled £421,430,131 and that these assets had an annual yield of £25,430,032. In 1835 Sir Robert Peel set up a Commission of Enquiry 'to consider the state of the Established Church with reference to Ecclesiastical Duties and Revenues'. The need for such an enquiry had been apparent for some time, since the finances of the great episcopal estates had become a source of considerable affluence to those fortunate enough to be called to apostolic office in the church,[10] whereas there were parish clergy living in poverty and it was proving impossible to find money for the endowment of new parishes called for by the burgeoning town populations. At this time there were no

[10] It has been estimated that the annual income of the Bishopric of Durham was at that time in excess of £500,000 in present day money.

central church finances – money was in the hands of some thousands of independent episcopal, cathedral and parochial corporations – and the nearest thing to a common fund was Queen Anne's Bounty, a charitable trust established during the early years of the previous century to improve the lot of the poorer clergy from ecclesiastical revenues which had previously been payable to the Crown. Sir Robert Peel's Commission of Enquiry consisted of seven government ministers, the Lord President of the Council, the two archbishops and three bishops. Immediately it encountered strong opposition – partly from the beneficiaries of the existing system, but mainly from conservative churchmen who were horrified at the prospect of the payment of the clergy being brought under some form of central control. In this they were reflecting the dislike of many Englishmen of a tendency towards centralization in government affairs. There was a further criticism: that the church was heavily outnumbered by Government representatives, but this was met by adding to the Commission all the bishops of England and Wales, three deans and two ecclesiastical judges. Unfortunately, the arrival of the bishops – many of whom were out of sympathy with the operation anyway – did not add to the efficiency of the Commission's activities, such as these were, and since the average attendance at meetings was only 10 or 11 out of a possible 49, effective power was in the hands of the full-time Secretary and his staff. In 1850 an Estates Committee was formed to manage the property acquired by the Commission, and three Church Estates Commissioners – two salaried, one not – were given complete control of all leasehold property. 'Enquiry' had given way to direct involvement in the management of property and the distribution of its revenues to poorer clergy and to those serving newly-formed parishes. Throughout the rest of the 19th century the Ecclesiastical Commissioners, as they came to be called, steadily acquired property and influence so that by the end of the century they were distributing £900,000 to more than 6,000 livings. Clergymen who had previously managed their own glebe or other forms of endowment found it more convenient – and in the end more profitable – to allow a central organization to handle these affairs.

The opportunities for the Ecclesiastical Commissioners to turn their assets to great gain were, however, somewhat limited. Many of their holdings were in agricultural land which yielded low rents, urban land had been let on 99-year leases so the rents did not advance with the general expansion of the country's economy, and investment was restricted to gilt-edged securities yielding modest returns. The Commissioners were in fact unable to meet all the demands which the Church of England made of them once it had to exist within a 20th-century economy. Speaking in the Church Assembly, on behalf of the Commissioners, in 1946, Sir Philip Baker Wilbraham said :

More and more of our surplus revenue (which, I grieve to say, shrinks year by year) has been used and spent as income. That means that for the moment a great deal more can be done with it, but when it is used, it is spent once and for all, and there is no addition to the resources of the church . . . Finally there is the reduction of interest on all our gilt-edged securities to a rate of 2½ per cent, which perhaps in some ways is the most crushing blow of all . . . In short every factor of the last ten years has been against us, and unless the Common Fund had been based on very strong and secure foundations it could not possibly have withstood the strain. The future is most uncertain, and in my opinion any policy of mortgaging the future for the present needs would be unsound.[11]

In the meantime Queen Anne's Bounty had been continuing along its elegantly benevolent path, until it received a windfall of £53 million in 1936 – the result of tithe redemption. It then became apparent that considerable advantages might accrue from an amalgamation of the Ecclesiastical Commissioners and Queen Anne's Bounty, although there were some who thought that the risk of over-centralization and bureaucracy would be reduced if the two bodies remained apart. In 1948 the amalgamation took place and the name-plate on the door

[11] Quoted by Mayfield, *op. cit.*, p. 135f.

of No. 1 Millbank was changed to the Church Commissioners for England. But, although the parties to the marriage were somewhat elderly and prim, and although their wedding had been 'arranged' by the Church Assembly, their new life together was vigorous and highly productive. Reserve funds were released for investment and a new policy was adopted, enabling commercial and industrial securities to replace the government stock which had by this time lost every trace of gilt. As the long leases came up for renewal, rents were raised to a realistic level or valuable urban land sold for redevelopment. Low yielding agricultural holdings were sold and the proceeds invested in more profitable enterprises, though the Church of England's traditional link with the countryside was preserved by the retention of more than 1,000 farms. During the first year of 'married' life the total income of the Church Commissioners was £7½ million. By 1961 this figure had been doubled and by 1971 it had been more than trebled to £25½ million. It may be presumed from this that over the past two decades the Commissioners have displayed considerable financial acumen, and there are few people in the 'city' ready to deny that they operate with consummate skill. Indeed, so successful have they been, and so grateful is the Church of England for the fruits of their labours, that even to question any aspect of their policy is to run the risk of being charged with blasphemy or indecency.

There are now 95 Church Commissioners and anyone who is tempted to believe that the Church of England is destined soon to become an instrument of revolutionary change in the country will do well to examine their names. The Queen appoints the First and Second Church Estates Commissioners and four other Commissioners. The Archbishop of Canterbury, who is in the chair, is supported by the Archbishop of York and the other 41 diocesan bishops. The Archbishop nominates four ordinary Commissioners and also the Third Church Estates Commissioner. *Ex officio* members include the Lord Chancellor, the First Lord of the Treasury, the Chancellor of the Exchequer, the Lord Chief Justice, the Master of the Rolls, the Attorney General and the Lord Mayors of Lon-

don and York. Two Commissioners are nominated by the
Aldermen of the City of London and two more by the
Vice-Chancellors of Oxford and Cambridge. Twenty-five
are appointed by the Church Assembly – two bishops,
three deans, two provosts, five archdeacons, two canons
and sundry laymen, including an earl, a baron and a
knight. It is not to be supposed, however, that every one
of the 95 is constantly scanning the columns of the
Financial Times. As many of them as can be mustered
are brought together for an annual meeting, but the real
decision-making is in the hands of two main committees
– the Assets Committee, which is responsible for handling
the investments, property and land (it met 20 times
during the year ended 31 March, 1971), and the General
Purposes Committee, which decides how the income from
the assets shall be spent (it met 9 times during the same
year). At this point a further qualification must be made
about decision-making. Although the main committees
meet quite frequently and can exercise a broad supervision of the Commissioner's affairs, the speed and special
skills demanded by many of the transactions make it
inevitable that great power should reside with the chief
administrators, in particular, the First and Third Estates
Commissioners, who are salaried officials and are, by law,
chairmen of all committees. The Assets Committee, made
up of four financial experts and one cleric, has

an exclusive power and duty to act on behalf and in the
name of the Commissioners in all matters relating both to
management of those assets of the Commissioners whose
income is carried into their general fund, including power to
sell, purchase, exchange or let land and make, realize and
change investments.

The powers and duties of this committee are such as
would overwhelm most ordinary mortals. On 31 March,
1971 they were responsible for assets whose total book
value was over £421$\frac{1}{4}$ million. During that year they
purchased about £20 million of Stock Exchange investments and sold about £17$\frac{1}{2}$ million, leaving them with
a portfolio valued at £208$\frac{1}{2}$ million. The income from this
source totalled £12$\frac{1}{2}$ million. Rental income from real
estate brought in £7$\frac{1}{2}$ million, which was about £$\frac{3}{4}$

million more than in the previous year, and, having sold 60 commercial properties for a total of more than £10 million (the largest being the Adelphi office block in the Strand), the committee invested £½ million in six others. Management of £31½ million of residential property obviously occupied a certain amount of time, but when the committee tired of city and urban air there were 166,208 acres of agricultural land to be visited (value £28½ million), and in fact 120 farms in seven counties saw something of the Commissioners during the year. Other farmers and their wives were entertained at receptions in Canterbury, Lincoln, Carlisle, Halsall and Cheltenham. Seven farm cottages were improved and the annual report notes that 'it was unnecessary to settle a rent by arbitration'. But soon it was time to return to the city to keep an eye on the Church Estates Development and Improvements Company which has £26 million invested in associated property companies and various other enterprises. It was a fairly busy year: the modernization of an office building in Regent Street was completed, the financing of industrial estates at Watford, Reading, Billericay, Abbotsinch and Smethwick continued, as did the extraction of sand and gravel from land owned by the Commissioners near Canterbury. Clearly this work-load could not easily have been carried by a committee of rural deans.

Nor could the rural deans have easily coped with the responsibilities of the General Purposes Committee, agreeable though it must be to spend over £25 million in twelve months. Here it has to be mentioned that the Committee is not allowed to allocate these funds to close relatives – or even to favourite charities. Acts of Parliament and Measures of Church Assembly specify precisely how the income of the Church Commissioners must be spent. By far the greater part must go to the payment of clergy stipends. Next comes the payment of clergy pensions and pensions to their widows. Assistance is to be given for the provision of suitable houses for the clergy, and grants may be made to meet gifts or bequests from the laity which are designed to endow benefices or provide parsonage houses. Last of all, a small amount may be devoted to church buildings in new housing areas and church schools. During the year 1970–71, 62.5 per cent went to clergy stipends, 11 per cent to pensions, 11.5 per cent to clergy houses, 3 per cent to new housing areas and church schools, while the remainder was shared between administration, reserves and addition to capital. Payments for parish clergy which totalled about £13¾ million, take the form of income from attached endowments, which vary considerably according to the history or good fortune of the parishes, and block grants to diocesan stipend funds which allow dioceses a certain degree of freedom in the disposal of the money. The bishops and their adminstrative expenses (including staff salaries) cost just over £700,000, cathedral clergy just under £1 million and archdeacons £145,000.

If this brief excursion into the realm of high finance suggests that the power and duty of the Church Commissioners are confined to monetary matters it is misleading. The Commissioners have a considerable interest in the pastoral work of the Church of England. One of their original functions was the re-defining of diocesan and parish boundaries, where this was considered necessary, and also the creation of new parishes. As far as can be ascertained, the Commissioners have pursued their acquisitive policies with such single-mindedness that, in a life of more than 120 years, they have yet to relinquish a single particle of power. Hence the meeting of the Pastoral Committee on 11 occasions during the year 1970–71, when consideration was given to a wide range of pastoral matters. Approval was given to the formation of three team ministries and three group ministries, to 73 schemes for uniting a total of 194 parishes, to 11 orders for the rearrangement of 48 rural deaneries, to 11 schemes for appropriating to other uses parts of churchyards, to 20 schemes involving the alteration of the boundaries of 61 parishes, to the plans of four churches intended to be parish churches, to the demolition of 15 disused churches, to 45 church redundancy declarations and so on. It is no part of the Commissioners' function to initiate pastoral reorganization but very little can be undertaken in this area of the Church of England's life without serious consideration being given to the question of what No. 1 Millbank might, or might not, be prepared to approve. It is reasonable to assume that they do not welcome innovation with open arms.

From time to time the Commissioners have been subjected to a certain amount of criticism, but it is not easy to discover the reasons which lie behind certain of their policies and, like the Treasury, they are not anxious to disclose much about their affairs. Valerie Pitt found it necessary to preface her interesting discussion of the subject with a warning:

The Church Commissioners are the most difficult subject I have ever had to write about partly because their structure and their work is complicated in itself, and partly because authentic, up-to-date information about it is very difficult to come by – at least, for publication. What is more, the Commissioners themselves are nervously sensitive to any flicker of inaccuracy, even in the choice of a word, even though they practise what Newman would have called 'reserve' about their affairs.[12]

Reticence over certain aspects of the operations of the multi-million-pound corporation functioning within a capitalist economy is of course quite understandable. Profits and disclosure rarely cohabit happily. Nonetheless it is hard to avoid the conclusion that the Church Commissioners withhold information of a certain kind, not because it would inhibit their speculative activities very seriously but because they believe that no one apart from themselves has the right to know. During the past few years, when there has been growing concern in Christian circles about the problems of race and world poverty, it has seemed proper to many churchmen to enquire about the investment policies of various companies and of the churches themselves. Are dividends being drawn from companies and enterprises which not only practise racial discrimination within the confines of their own activities but also bolster up a system which makes it possible for exploitation to continue? Is an adequate proportion of investment going to developing countries where so many

12 *Prism Pamphlet* No. 36.

human lives depend upon an inflow of capital? These questions are neither trivial nor impertinent and the asking of them in the United States has led to radical changes in the investment policies of the largest American churches. Yet it is virtually impossible to discover how much, if any, of the Commissioners' capital is invested in areas of racial tension or indeed in any other part of the globe. The 1971 report disclosed that for the first time an investment of £2¼ million had been made in the stocks of companies in the United States, and the 1970 report commented on a Church Assembly debate of the previous year in which questions had been raised about the investment policy of the Church of England:

The Commissioners undertook to review the extent to which their investments already assist developing countries, and to consider whether there is scope for increasing these investments without breaching their statutory duties towards the clergy. It has been estimated that some £18 million, representing 8.7 per cent of their total Stock Exchange portfolio, can already be regarded as being invested indirectly in the poorer developing countries. As regards a possible increase in the scale of this investment, active negotiations in progress at the end of the year have led to the Commissioners subscribing £1 million for an 8 per cent Debenture (partly convertible) in the Commonwealth Development Finance Company Ltd. This investment will provide 'new' capital for the developing countries whilst ensuring to the Commissioners security of capital and an acceptable return.

These are tiny morsels of information, and if the Commissioners have nothing to hide there seems no reason why further disclosures should not be forthcoming, but there are revealing phrases in the 1970 statement which indicate the tension in which (hopefully) the Commissioners always operate. It is their duty to preserve their capital intact and to secure from it the best possible return for the benefit of the clergy. They are therefore inhibited from running high risks and discouraged from investing in enterprises which, however worthy in themselves, are unlikely to yield rich dividends. It is taken for granted that they will not invest in activities which are known to be socially harmful. But serious questions have been raised about housing development policies which, at a time of chronic housing shortage for the underprivileged section of British society, enable the Church Commissioners to invest in the Hyde Park Water Garden project which provides luxury accommodation for people in the £10,000 a year income bracket. The Commissioners reply that this development has absorbed only a small part of their investments, that they are involved in a large number of projects which provide housing for poor people and that, in the final resort, the clergy will have to meet the cost of large-scale transfers of funds from reasonably profitable to less profitable enterprises.

Given the Commissioners' terms of reference, such a reply is not unreasonable. But it raises more fundamental questions about their terms of reference and their relationship to the Church of England as a whole. Although the church is well represented in the Church Commissioners by the bishops and by elected members of the General Synod, the history of the Commissioners and the nature of their activities have combined to make them, in effect, an autonomous body. Legally, the General Synod may pass Measures which, if given parliamentary approval, can give directions to the Commissioners and even secure changes in policy, yet rarely are their affairs discussed in the councils of the Church of England and, even when they are, the Commissioners are treated with the reverence and awe normally reserved for a wealthy and munificent aunt who must be humoured at all times and never given the slightest excuse for offence. This means that the General Synod, which is elected to direct the central government of the Church of England, has no effective control over almost half the funds which are available for disposal from central sources. As Miss Pitt pointed out, the position is analogous to one in which the Treasury had complete control of half the funds in the national exchequer and was not subject to parliamentary questioning or any discernible political influence. History shows clearly how this situation has arisen in the relationship between the Church Commissioners and the government of the Church of England, but a decision is now required as to whether it shall be allowed to continue. The Archbishops' Advisers have given irrefutable evidence that the financial pressure on the church will reach crisis proportions during the next five years. It is obviously appropriate that church members should be challenged to demonstrate their commitment by means of more generous giving. But an increasing number of Anglicans will first need to be assured that their church's existing resources are being wisely deployed and also that funds are under some form of corporate control. If, as seems more than likely, the shape of the Church of England in the years to come is to be determined more by financial considerations than by theological insight, it is essential that the purse strings shall be held by those who represent the mind of the whole church (so far as this can be ascertained), who have an over-view of the whole of the church's changing needs, and who are accountable to the whole church for whatever actions they choose to take.

chapter 9

Influence and
Influencers

Any society wishing to devise a system of government that would guarantee it immunity from dictatorship or any form of oligarchic rule could hardly do better than examine the Church of England. While allowing those to whom it entrusts leadership a degree of freedom – which encourages something akin to autocracy – within certain defined areas, it is careful to ensure that the power and influence of any single bishop, priest or layman is never able to spill over into the church at large. There is, in consequence, not the slightest risk of the Church of England succumbing to the charms of a demagogue or of creating any institutionalized leadership form which even faintly resembles the papacy. Nonetheless, behind the formidable resources and organization of the Church of England there are real people, some of whom have greater responsibilities and influence than others, most of whom have far less power and influence than is commonly supposed.

No clearer illustration of this can be seen than that provided by the Archbishopric of Canterbury. Although the occupant of the chair of St. Augustine is titled Metropolitan of All England, is regarded as *primus inter pares* of the entire Anglican Communion, and occupies a place of great prominence in the life of church and state, his effective writ runs no further than the boundaries of the Diocese of Canterbury, which do not even embrace the whole of the County of Kent. He may visit other dioceses at the invitation of their bishops or, if he so chooses and has the necessary time, carry out an official visitation within the Province of Canterbury (except the

Diocese of London), but no one is obliged to take the slightest notice of his advice, appeals or threats unless they happen to be contravening the law in the matter. When a bishopric is vacant, the archbishop becomes responsible for its spiritual oversight – a function he is normally only too pleased to delegate to another bishop on the spot – but he has no claim upon the revenues of the See and exercises no more control over the clergy and laity of the diocese than the bishop-retired or the bishop-elect – which means very little indeed. Discussing his position generally, the present Archbishop of Canterbury, Dr. Michael Ramsey, pointed out in 1971[1] that although his personal responsibilities had increased considerably during the ten years he had lived in Lambeth Palace, his power had, with the growth of synodical government, actually decreased. The responsibilities to which the Archbishop was referring were not of an administrative character but those which come with increased exposure to the public eye through the mass media and involve an individual in accepting a representative role on behalf of his institution and, in this case, on behalf of the Christian religion. As Bishop Barry has pointed out: ' " A lead from the church " has now become rather a cliché, and means in effect a speech by an archbishop.'[2] A feature of Dr. Ramsey's primacy so far has been his marked reluctance to make public utterances unless he actually has something to say. He has little social small-talk and would certainly support the mediaeval teacher who instructed his pupils: 'Do not speak unless you can improve on the silence.' The Archbishop is in fact a mixture of the mediaeval and the modern, of the patriarch and the don. No one has yet claimed to have forecast during the 1940s and early 1950s that the man who was successively a Professor of Divinity at Durham and the Regius Professor of Divinity at Cambridge would one day become the 100th Archbishop of Canterbury. Dr. Ramsey, the author of a very influential book *The Gospel and the Catholic Church*, was the archetypal professor—

[1] In a conversation with the author.
[2] *Period of My Life* by F. R. Barry, p. 157, Hodder & Stoughton 1971.

meticulous in scholarship and engagingly eccentric in manner. But just beneath the surface of the don was a devout high churchman who moved with consummate ease into episcopal office in 1952 and whose appearance at his enthronement in Durham Cathedral created an illusion that the pages of history had been turned back to the 13th century. He loved Durham and Durham loved him, though the younger clergy of the diocese were aware that his massive frame housed not only a radical mind but also a conservative heart. Members of the Parish and People movement were somewhat disturbed when, at their annual conference held in Durham, he warned them of certain dangers he perceived in the development of the Parish Communion. It seemed as if a somewhat old-fashioned high churchman was still opting for a Low Mass at 8 a.m. and a non-communicating High Mass at 11. When Dr. Cyril Garbett died on the last day of 1955, shortly before his announced retirement, Durham knew that it must inevitably lose its bishop to the Archbishopric of York; he was enthroned in York Minster in May. Well before Dr. Geoffrey Fisher's long-awaited retirement was announced there was speculation as to whether Ramsey (his former pupil at Repton) would be his successor at Canterbury. Members of the inner ecclesiastical circle knew that Fisher wanted Donald Coggan, the much less complicated and more predictable Bishop of Bradford, to succeed him and was trying to influence the Prime Minister in this direction, but the majority of the Bench of Bishops recognized Ramsey's depth and subtle wisdom, and he moved to Canterbury in 1961. He was, in fact, the only serious runner but there were questions in some minds (especially Fisher's) about his administrative skill and his vigour. His arrival on the national scene occasioned some surprise among the general public who found it difficult to believe that he was not older than the outgoing Primate and who wondered why the leadership of the national church in the 20th century had been entrusted to someone who appeared to have been resurrected from a distant ecclesiastical past. But television viewers quickly came to recognize in the new Archbishop a man of formidable intellect,

F

simple faith, utter integrity and warm humanity –
qualities not lightly to be dismissed in any public figure.
As the years have passed, so he has grown in stature
until he now has an unrivalled position in the life of the
Church of England. In the General Synod, as in the
Church Assembly, he stands head and shoulders above
every other member, and unfortunate is the man or
woman who is called to speak after him. But a continuous
battle is going on between the conservative patriarch
and the radical don. The cool reception given to the
Parish Communion development has been repeated whenever some new approach has been mooted – from House
Churches through *Honest to God* to financial support for
freedom fighting movements in Southern Africa – but
once the Archbishop's mind has had opportunity to
wrestle with the issues, and is satisfied of the coherence
and integrity of the proposals, he emerges as the cham-
pion of reform. This has often been a tiresome experience
for the reformers but Michael Ramsey's initial scepticism
has sometimes enabled him to win support for change
from quarters that would never have responded to the
call of the initiating radicals. As a disciple of William
Temple, he has always taken the nation's social and
political problems seriously, and without ever revealing
his mentor's political flair and sensitivity, has established
in the House of Lords a tradition that the bishops may
always be expected to support the liberal approach and
solution. In the light of the reactionary image reflected
by the episcopal bench for the greater part of English
history, this has been no mean achievement. No Archbishop of Canterbury has travelled further and more
frequently in the Anglican Communion, and the patriarch
has often indulged himself – as well as discharged his
duty – with visits to the leaders of the Orthodox churches
of the East, with whom he has many spiritual and theological affinities. At the Vatican and at the headquarters
of the World Council of Churches he is viewed with some
suspicion, but he probably regards this as a sign of grace.
The two real weaknesses of his Primacy so far have been
those which caused his old headmaster to suppose, mistakenly, that he was unfitted for Lambeth – administrative

inadequacy and a certain lethargy. He makes no secret of the fact that he hates councils and committees and is bored stiff with the desk work which inevitably goes with his job, the efficient discharge of which can make a considerable difference to the life of the church. Although the administrative load has become increasingly heavy during the past 50 years, there has never been anything faintly resembling a curial office at Lambeth Palace and the past decade has seen a depressing series of weak appointments to the Archbishop's personal staff, with the result that work either could not, or would not, be delegated. In this situation, his relaxed approach has probably saved his life. Any man who threw himself whole-heartedly into the administrative chores – as Fisher did – and at the same time took time for reflection and study, besides all the other duties of the office, would certainly be inviting an early breakdown. But Ramsey has a remarkable ability to 'switch off' when he has had enough and, although the result has been a style of leadership less than dynamic, there has been an important benefit in that during a period of great debate about the reform of church life, and the relationship of the church to secular society, the Church of England has never been allowed to forget the priority of the spiritual and transcendental elements in its work. In November 1972 he was 68 and ready for retirement to the house which has already been acquired for the purpose in Cuddesdon. But in the absence of a suitable successor, it seems necessary for him to soldier on for a few more years until certain younger bishops have matured in the episcopate and certain older ones have been phased out.

The problem of the administrative arrangements at Lambeth, which have been a source of concern since the premature death of William Temple in 1944, cannot be isolated from the question of who will be at the helm for the next phase of the Church of England's history. When Dr. Maurice Harland, who had succeeded Michael Ramsey at Durham, announced his retirement in 1966 there was the usual speculation about who would be appointed to a bishopric which, by reason of its traditions, enjoys a certain pre-eminence. Among the names canvassed, few

included that of the Nolloth Professor of the Philosophy
of the Christian Religion at Oxford, but when the appointment of Dr. Ian T. Ramsey (no relation of the Archbishop)
was announced it was immediately recognized as an inspired choice. Small of stature and speaking in an un-
fashionable Lancastrian accent, Ian Ramsey gave an initial
impression of an affable North-country rural dean. But
the impression was short-lived; as soon as he moved into
action it became apparent that a mind of outstanding
quality was at work – a mind able to engage the attention
of distinguished scientists, physicians, philosophers and
politicians and of relating theological insights to their
areas of concern. Yet Ian Ramsey moved with equal ease
at a party following a village Confirmation. It was a rare
and engaging combination of gifts and such a combination
was exceedingly vulnerable to exploitation once its owner
had been raised to an episcopal bench where talent –
especially of the intellectual sort – was at a premium.
Soon the Bishop of Durham was in the chair of the permanent and important Commission on Doctrine; next he was
landed with the chairmanship of a high-powered Commission on Religious Education in Schools; then came the
chairmanship of the Central Religious Advisory Council
which advises both the B.B.C. and the I.B.A. on religious
broadcasting policy. As if this and a large industrial diocese were not enough to absorb his energy, he accepted
a heavy programme of conferences, lectures and overseas
tours and by 1970 it was clear that anyone undertaking
so much, with the assistance only of a chaplain and a
secretary, must sooner or later collapse under the strain.
The first heart attack came on Easter Eve 1972 and,
although a summer convalescence promised a good recovery, Ian Ramsey was quickly back to his usual
programme of work and the second heart attack in
October 1972 proved to be fatal. This was a devastating
blow to the Church of England for not only had it lost
its most able bishop, it had also been deprived of the only
serious contender for the Archbishopric of Canterbury
when Michael Ramsey offered his resignation – probably
in 1973. In retrospect it can be seen that even had Ian
Ramsey gone to Canterbury a man of his temperament,

who could never decline an invitation, would have been unable to survive the constant pressures of the office.

One bishop who would have no difficulty in sorting out the administrative problems – though he is unlikely to be given the opportunity of doing so – is Dr. Gerald Ellison, whose entry in *Who's Who* reveals the classic background of a Church of England bishop:

CHESTER, Bishop of, since 1955; Rt. Rev. Gerald Alexander Ellison; b. 19 Aug. 1910; s. of Late Preb. John Henry Joshua Ellison, C.V.O., Chaplain in Ordinary to the King, Rector of St. Michael's, Cornhill, and of Sara Dorothy Graham Ellison (née Crum); m. 1947, Jane Elizabeth, d. of late Brig. John Houghton Gibbon, D.S.O.; one s. two d. Educ.: St. George's, Windsor; Westminster School; New Coll., Oxford; Westcott House, Cambridge. Curate, Sherborne Abbey, 1935–37; Domestic Chaplain to the Bishop of Winchester, 1937–39; Chaplain, R.N.V.R., 1940-43 (despatches); Domestic Chaplain to Archbishop of York, 1943-46; Vicar of St. Mark's, Portsea, 1946-50; Canon of Portsmouth, 1950; Examining Chaplain to Bishop of Portsmouth 1949-50; Bishop Suffragan of Willesden, 1950-55; Select Preacher: Oxford University, 1940 and 1961, Cambridge University, 1957; Chaplain, Master Mariners' Company, 1946; Chaplain, Glass Sellers' Company, 1951; Chaplain and Sub-Prelate, Order of St. John, Mem. Wolfenden Cttee. on Sport, 1960; Chm. Westfield Coll., University of London; *Publications*: The Churchman's Duty, 1957; The Anglican Communion, 1960. *Recreations*: oarsmanship, walking. *Address*: Bishop's House, Chester. *Clubs*: Athenaeum, Leander.

The most significant pieces of biography here are the periods spent as Domestic Chaplain to the Bishop of Winchester and as Domestic Chaplain to the Archbishop of York. In both instances the chaplaincy was to Cyril Forster Garbett, who left a deep mark on Ellison, as indeed he did on all his chaplains. It was the mark of what can best be described as ruthless Anglicanism. Its basis lies in a deep love of, and dependence on, the Church of England as it has taken shape over the centuries. Upon this is built an aggressive determination that, by dint of hard work and good organization, the inherited structure of church life shall be made to function with the

utmost efficiency. The results can sometimes be impressive – as in the case of the famous parish of St. Mary,
Portsea, under Garbett's leadership during the early years
of the century, and even today in certain places – but
the approach is essentially conservative for it will not
permit any reform that threatens to change the character
of the inheritance. Hence the image of the Bishop of
Chester who can happily take part in the launching of a
Polaris nuclear submarine but cannot bear the thought
of a parson losing his freehold. To suggest that Dr. Ellison
was responsible for the rejection of the Morley Report
proposals, which offered the Church of England the possibility of real reformation, would be to credit him with
more influence than he actually possesses, but his own
'alternative report', and interventions in the Church
Assembly debate, provided a rallying point for the conservative elements in the Church of England, and his
skilful handling of the official procedures secured the
downfall of Morley. This provoked the Bishop of Guildford (Dr. George Reindorp) to observe, 'The Bishop of
Chester, like most oarsmen, believes that he can only
move forward by looking backward.' Evidently many
church leaders received their early training on the river.

This was not the case with Dr. John Robinson, who
moved away from the ecclesiastical centre when he
became Dean of Chapel at Trinity College, Cambridge in
1969, but had by then made a deep dent in the traditional
theological teaching of the Church of England and of
most of the other English churches. Looking back to 1963
it now seems astonishing that so modest a theological
essay as *Honest to God* should have created such a sen-
sation and that more than a million copies in seventeen
different languages should have been sold in less than a
decade. But, as Dr. Robinson himself has pointed out,
'It is a safe assumption that a best-seller tells one more
about the state of the market than the quality of the
product.'[3] Which is not to say that *Honest to God* was
not a good book. The Archbishop of Canterbury declared
it to be 'muddled', without apparently noticing that the

[3] *The Honest to God Debate* by John A. T. Robinson and David L.
Edwards, p. 233, SCM Press, 1963.

same could be said of many books in the Bible and much of the best Christian writing across the ages. Professor Christopher Evans was correct in placing *Honest to God* in the Devotional section of his library[4] for it was the attempt of a man confined to bed with a slipped disc 'simply to be honest about what God means to me – in the second half of the twentieth century.'[5] There were many different elements in the market which demanded so many copies of the bishop's reflections, of which the chief was clearly the repressed disbelief of many ordinary Christians in the traditional dogmas offered by their churches. Bishop Robinson was coming to terms with a personal dilemma but he was also aware, after working for four years in one of the most intractable mission areas in Europe, that the kind of things being spoken from pulpits and at other places of Christian assembly were no longer meaningful to the overwhelming mass of the people. His episcopal colleagues had, it appears, not cottoned on to this fact and one of the most depressing factors in the violent reaction to the publication of *Honest to God* was the number of bishops who denounced the book without having taken the trouble to read it. This was in itself symptomatic of something even more depressing: the inability or unwillingness of a large proportion of the church's leadership to keep in touch with developments in the realm of theological reflection. There was very little in *Honest to God* that was new. John Robinson brought together into a somewhat uneasy synthesis the main thoughts of three major 20th century theologians – Paul Tillich, Rudolph Bultmann and Dietrich Bonhoeffer – whose written work had been available for a decade and more. Yet few English churchmen, apart from a handful of professional theologians, had taken the trouble to read them; hence the bombshell effect of *Honest to God* on the Church of England. Ten years later it seems that at least some of the thinking of these and other continental theologians has begun to seep into the episcopal consciousness, though it is but rarely reflected in the teaching and preaching of the bishops. John

---

[4] *ibid*, p. 111.
[5] John Robinson in an article in the *Sunday Mirror*, 7 April 1963.

Robinson is himself a professional theologian, as the long list of his writings clearly indicates, but the fact that he is also a great pastor and a gifted communicator at many different levels has so far diverted him from the continuous, disciplined and meticulous work that goes into the writing of a major theological work. While the storms raged around the publication of *Honest to God*, its author was quietly conducting Confirmations, instituting new vicars and ministering to individuals in South London. When he took time off to write articles or other books their impact was heightened by the powerful prose in which they appeared – either in a learned theological journal or in a popular tabloid newspaper. As in the case of Ian Ramsey, the combination of gifts is an unusual one and this raises the question of how such a man can best serve the church. During his last two years as Bishop of Woolwich it became clear that he had ceased to be regarded as the Church of England's 'naughty boy'. His contributions to the debates of the Church Assembly were listened to with increasing respect and often earned great applause. When the time came for him to go, he was accepted – though by no means absorbed. The move from South London to Cambridge seemed strange in many ways, and was mistakenly interpreted by some as a deliberate abandoning of the Church of England's structure, but after ten years of grinding pastoral work and the intense mental and emotional strain of public controversy it was neither surprising nor improper that he should be drawn towards a more relaxed atmosphere. The big question now is whether Dr. Robinson can make his best contribution to the life of the church by remaining in a place of influence which also offers space for reflection, or whether, at the age of 53, there is still an opportunity for the Church of England to use his gifts in one of its more important bishoprics. He may not feel that they should be so used, but it will be a serious reflection on the sensitivity and prodigality of the Church of England if no attempt is made to harness such talent to the service of its institutional life during a time of deepening crisis.

Peers of the Realm have served the Church of England in many different ways over the course of the centuries

and, since the advent of representative church government, a number of them have played a prominent part in
the church's councils. Given the deep conservatism of the
English aristocracy, there are ample grounds for supposing that these men would not be prominent among those
Anglicans who are anxious to introduce their church to
the harsh realities of 20th century life. But a notable
exception is to be seen in the 44-year-old Earl of March
and Kinrara who is now one of the Church of England's
leading and most forward-looking laymen. As heir to the
Duke of Richmond, his early years were appropriately
orthodox – Eton – but then, instead of the predictable
season at Oxford, he qualified as a Chartered Accountant
and soon became involved in the important frontier work
of William Temple College, Rugby. At the same time he
threw in his lot with the reforming and renewing efforts
of the Parish and People movement, and so became identified with the radical wing of the Church of England. In
1960 Chichester diocese elected him as one of the
youngest members of the Church Assembly and since
that time his responsibilties and influence have grown
rapidly. He became a Church Commissioner in 1963 and
now serves as a member of the small specialist group
which advises the archbishops on the Church of England's
needs and resources. He was vice-chairman of the Chadwick Commission on Church and State and is now chairman of the General Synod's important Board for Mission
and Unity. His interests in the wider church are reflected
in membership of the Central Committee of the World
Council of Churches and the Church of England's Council
on Foreign Relations. Obviously, this amount of responsibility could only be assumed by someone with freedom to order his time to meet a great variety of
commitments. While men of the calibre and outlook of
the Earl of March are available to undertake work of this
kind, the Church of England can count itself fortunate,
but there remains unanswered an important question
concerning how reasonably typical laymen can ever be
expected to shoulder major responsibilities in the central
government of their church when the demands on time
are so considerable – and so expensive.

In 1972 only the River Thames separated the locations of the Church of England's two best-known Canons – Ronald Jasper of Westminster Abbey and Eric James of Southwark Cathedral – but the gulf between their respective approaches to the church's current problems is almost as wide as infinity. Both began their ministries in an unspectacular fashion and both had the disadvantage (for an Anglican) of a 'red brick' education. Jasper was a curate in Durham, moved to a chaplaincy at University College, Durham and then became vicar of a country parish on Teesside. James was a curate in London, moved to a chaplaincy at Trinity College, Cambridge, and then became vicar of a tough urban parish in Camberwell. But during these early years each was developing his own special interest and at the same time was being moulded by his concern. Ronald Jasper had read history at Leeds, showed a flair for patient research and devoted a good deal of his free time on Teesside to tracing the pattern of Prayer Book revision in the Church of England and to examining the papers of A. C. Headlam, who had been one of the most influential church leaders of the inter-war years and died in 1947. Two books on liturgical revision were the result and also a fine biography of Headlam. Eric James had already begun to display marked pastoral gifts and an enquiring mind while reading theology at London, and his subsequent experience drove him to a deep desire that the pattern of the church's life might be changed so that care could be shown to individuals in their own milieu. Two books – one on sacramental confession, the other on the role of the priest in 20th-century society – reflected his concern and the title of the book on priesthood, *Odd Man Out*, confirmed that he was moving towards radical solutions of pastoral problems. Jasper's work had caused him to think seriously about the past, James could not forget the present and the future.

Thus disposed, the two men moved into key positions during the 1960s – Ronald Jasper to the heart of the church establishment, with the chairmanship of the Liturgical Commission and a Canonry at Westminster; Eric James to the fringe, with the Directorship of Parish and People, a temporary home and an uncertain income.

Jasper has played, and will continue to play, a crucial part in the revision of the Church of England's forms of worship. He must work with a Commission and all suggestions must be submitted to the untutored members of the General Synod, but the chairman, by reason of his expertise and continuous attention to the matter in hand, must inevitably have a dominating influence over the revised services that eventually find their way into the worship of the parish churches. Of Dr. Jasper's knowledge of the history of Anglican liturgy and of the current developments in other churches there cannot be the slightest doubt. But his approach is essentially academic, in the pejorative sense of the word, and seeks the perfection of something which the church has inherited in an unsatisfactory form from the past. He could not say, with Eric James, 'Liturgy is not something which can be talked of by the church as though it merely involved its own society. The roots of the liturgy are in the ground of society',[6] and it is significant that Jasper's biography of the wide-ranging Bishop George Bell was much less satisfactory than his earlier work on the essentially ecclesiastical Bishop Headlam. The Westminster Abbey canonries provide a good base for certain forms of specialist activity, but the beautiful Little Cloister looks a trifle too safe for the production of creative liturgy related not only to the past but also to the turbulent present.

Eric James became Director of Parish and People in 1964, soon after this movement had joined forces with the Keble Conference Group and secured sufficient resources to employ a full-time official. Parish and People was already fifteen years old and, with the Parish Communion well established in the life of the Church of England, the early 1960s were devoted mainly to discussions of whether or not the movement, which was noticeably running out of steam, should gracefully fold up. The Keble Conference Group, on the other hand, had only been born in 1961 and its membership included most of the young, radical clergymen who had been ordained in the late 1950s and were determined to change the structures of the Church of England. This was a brief era

6 *The Roots of the Liturgy* by Eric James, p. 2, Prism Pamphlet, 1962.

which, in retrospect, appears to have been an Indian summer for the church. The number of Confirmation candidates and, more significantly, the number of ordinations began to rise. Parish clergy spoke of increasing congregations and a new breed of clerics – whose numbers included men of considerable ability – believed that the Church of England was ripe for a new reformation. There was hope that Mervyn Stockwood, who had recently moved from Cambridge to Southwark and attracted to his diocese a band of able – even if somewhat noisy – priests, might lead a successful onslaught on the hitherto intractable problems of South London. An editorial in the *Church of England Newspaper* in 1960 informed its readers that 'A new Church of England is being born, a church efficient, sophisticated and progressive, a church with money enough and to spare.' On the eve of his retirement from Canterbury, Archbishop Fisher announced that the Church of England was 'in good heart'.

Against this background, the merging of Parish and People and the Keble Conference Group was seen by the leaders of the two bodies as providing an opportunity for the launching of a new 'Life and Liberty' movement. A comprehensive programme of reform was hammered out. This showed the new 'Parish and People' to be concerned for synodical government, the proper deployment and payment of the clergy, liturgical reform, Baptismal discipline, team and group ministries, industrial mission and lay education. There was some debate, and disagreement, over the question of whether the movement should become 'political' by encouraging and supporting reformers who might seek election to the Church Assembly. The old Parish and People hands were unhappy about this, fearing that it might revive the 'party' spirit in the church's councils, but in the end a significant number of members were elected to the Assembly and made a strong contribution to its life over a period of five years. Whenever commissions had to be appointed, it was necessary to take account of this element in the Assembly and provide an appropriate number of places for them. The monthly magazine *Prism*, succeeded in 1965 by the fortnightly *New Christian*, provided a public platform which attracted the attention of 10,000 readers in 1966. Meanwhile, Eric James was touring the country, addressing meetings, encouraging the formation of Parish and People groups in the dioceses, writing articles and playing a personal part in the Church Assembly's commissions and committees. About 2,000 people became subscribing members of Parish and People but there were many more sympathizers who attended meetings and bought literature. A stimulating conference, under the title 'The World is the Agenda', was held in Birmingham in 1966 and in the same year Eric James began to combine his work with a residentiary canonry of Southwark Cathedral. The Birmingham conference marked a change of mood among the most influential leaders of Parish and People, who became increasingly concerned with the life of the secular community rather than that of the ecclesiastical community. This was due, in part, to impatience with the slow pace of reform in the Church of England, but mainly to a recognition of the fact that the life of the church cannot be considered in isolation from the world in which it is set and to which it is called to minister. By 1968, many of the reforms proposed by Parish and People were under consideration by the church at large and some were in process of implementation, but it now became painfully clear that, while the Church of England was undoubtedly changing, the world was changing much more quickly and that, in spite of a major effort for reform and renewal, the church was becoming even more marginal to the real concerns of the English people. Eric James resigned from the Directorship in that year, in order to devote himself to the inner-city areas of South London, and although the movement struggled on for a further two years its membership and enthusiasm were in decline and it was with a yawn of relief that it sank its identity into a new coalition of tired denominational renewal groups which came together to form 'One for Christian Renewal' in 1970. Eric James, in common with many of his former colleagues in Parish and People, now sees his main work as lying, not within the Church of England's machinery of organization but at one or more of the points of intersection between church and society.

The number of church leaders who can operate effectively at any of these points of intersection remains small. While the present Bench of bishops is not over-stocked with talent, it can be said that virtually every one of its members has a strong pastoral sensitivity and could be relied upon to show the utmost care for any individual – priest or layman – who sought his help. In this sense, all are very good bishops. But if the Church of England still believes itself to be the church of the English people, and to have a responsibility towards the whole of society, the pastoral duties of a bishop cannot be considered solely in terms of care for individuals – important though this obviously is. Pastoral care in the 20th century is to be exercised through a relationship with many different organs of society, the majority of them of secular constitution, which exercise responsibility for individuals in a great variety of ways. Yet the church leaders who have any real grasp of the way in which a technologically-dominated society functions and coheres can be counted on the fingers of one hand. This is one more sign of the crisis in which the Church of England is now immersed. Its ethos and outlook is that of an agrarian age and until an urban-orientated leadership has begun to emerge the danger of the church being regarded in-creasingly as a curiosity from the past will not be dis-pelled.

chapter 10

Reality and Locality

The crisis now facing the Church of England is
not a new one. It has been there ever since England
became an industrial society, though sometimes it has
been masked by factors which could not be accurately
interpreted at the time and, more frequently, it has been
denied by a stubborn refusal to face facts. The difference today is that many of these facts are making their
presence felt more powerfully and those who have not
dismissed them as an illusion or not chosen to look in
another direction are aware of the crisis, and are also
aware that the crisis is now rapidly deepening. Having
acknowledged that the crisis is not a new one, it is also
necessary to recognize that it touches the heart of the
Church of England's life. Many of the most dangerous
problems now facing the Church of England derive from
the very basis of its institutional shape as this evolved
during the Middle Ages and took distinctive form at the
Reformation. Those who are resistant to certain changes
because they believe these will change the character of
the Church of England are certainly correct in their assessment, even if they are misguided in their resistance.

Preoccupation with history is a fatal trap, but those
who are concerned with the future of institutions cannot
afford to ignore history, neither can they neglect the hard
facts of institutional life. Even a nodding acquaintance
with these two areas of knowledge will show the reformer
of the Church of England that revolutionary change is
impossible and immediate collapse almost equally so. This
stability – frustrating for some, comforting for others –
cannot be attributed either to corruption or to Divine
protection. It is simply (though the factors are in fact
highly complex) that an institution of great antiquity has

over the course of the centuries devised ways of protect-
ing itself against rapid change and also against destruc-
tion. Conservation and conservatism have more than
linguistic affinities. Reforming England's national church
is just as difficult as is the reforming of England's parliamentary and judicial institutions, and in every case the
problems are remarkably similar.

Looking to the future, therefore, it would be wise to
assume that the Church of England will still be in evidence
at the turn of the 21st century, which is now less than
three decades away. There is a good chance that it will
still be around at the turn of the 22nd century, though
long-range projections of this kind are hardly helpful. A
30-year period is rather more manageable. But even a
period of reform extending over 30 years will be too
long for many of the Church of England's liveliest spirits.
They have, as they are wont to say, 'only one life to
live' and the prospect of devoting the greater part of it to
the task of freeing the limbs of an elderly and arthritic
maiden aunt is far from alluring. They will, in these circumstances, move to the fringes of the Church of England's life and give themselves to forms of work which
are more obviously improving the lot of humanity, either
in Britain or, increasingly, in other parts of the world.
Their going, while causing regret at the personal level,
should occasion neither disappointment nor recrimina-
tion. If the church is committed to the service of the
Kingdom of God, it can hardly complain if some of its
best members devote themselves totally to that service
outside the confines of ecclesiastical life and influence.
Given the Church of England's historic commitment to
the life of national and local communities, it would not
be unreasonable to suppose that those who feel called to
maintain the ecclesiastical institution might extend a
supporting and understanding hand to any who move to
the fringe and who wish to maintain some form of contact with their origins. Obviously the church cannot keep
attached to its apron strings those who wish to become
entirely free, but the special challenge of the present
moment is to show acceptance and love towards those
who choose new, and possibly unorthodox, paths of

service. This means ceasing to regard the priest who moves out of the parochial ministry as an outsider; it means resisting the temptation to suppose that a layman or laywoman whose links with the church have become tenuous is no more than a cowardly deserter.

The next thirty years also seem certain to see an increase in the number of Anglicans who, while keeping one foot firmly inside the institutional church, find their main work and fulfilment outside it. This is, of course, the position of the overwhelming majority of the laity already. The new factor is that they are being joined by some of the clergy who are seeking ways of exercising their priesthood in a variety of secular spheres, ranging from the factory floor, through community and social work, to a directorship of a First Division football club. Such people frequently find themselves convening or join- ing groups of Christians who are in a similar situation and who do not find the liturgical and community life of the church providing them with adequate support for their work in the world. Hence the proliferation of what the Archbishop of Canterbury has called 'experimental church life', expressed when Christians gather informally in houses or elsewhere for worship, reflection, prayer and service. Many of these groups are ephemeral – meeting the needs of their members for a time, then dissolving – but they are extremely important pointers towards the future shape of a church which will have far fewer build- ings than at present and will be far less dependent upon buildings for its work. Vocational, project-orientated, neighbourhood, community service and other groups suggest patterns of church life which could run parallel to the more formal structures and in some areas replace them. Again, it is important that contact should be main- tained – in some places, established – between those who remain firmly within the life of the parish church and those whose attachment is to something smaller, less formal and more intense. These are not schismatics or promoters of splinter-groups, but Christians involved in important experiments which have something to teach the whole church. Contact can of course only be maintained if the experimenters are prepared to acknowledge that those who do not join them, apparently remaining firmly wedded to the old ways, are not necessarily back-woodsmen who have no vision. Among them are many Christians of deep spirituality and holiness of life who, for many different reasons, find it impossible to let go of the inheritance which over the years has been the source of their strength and inspiration. Whatever the weaknesses of the church in the past and the present, the fact remains that almost every Christian has received his or her knowledge of Christ through the church. The vessel may have been earthen, but it still carried a treasure and not everyone finds it possible to abandon or smash the vessel so long as there remains the possibility of using it for a little longer.

How best can it be used in the present situation? Two facts offer encouragement and incentive. The resources of the Church of England are still massive and provide a unique network of bases for work in every part of the country. Many of the church's buildings are a major problem, yet the machinery of the church supports and connects many thousands of communities of people who are motivated by high ideals and are committed to dedicated service. It is quite impossible to over-estimate the potentiality embodied in these communities. Furthermore, there is ample evidence to show that when there is imaginative leadership it is still possible for local churches in many – though not all – areas to exhibit a vigorous life which is closely related to the needs of individuals and communities. A great deal of the organizational life of the church stands in need of reform, and inadequate central government can easily inhibit local freedom, but there are still many opportunities awaiting those parish churches which are ready to seize them. Lack of vision and sensitivity is a more serious problem for the Church of England today than administrative inefficiency. The aim must be to turn England's parish churches into centres of reflection, reconciliation, celebration and concern for the underprivileged.[1] This will not necessarily lead to an increase in the size of con-

[1] The implications of this are discussed further in the author's book *An Eye for an Ear*, SCM Press, 1972.

gregations or to a broad smile on the face of every treasurer, but a four-fold programme of this kind will enable the church to offer something distinctive and highly relevant in every community.

Needless to say, it is easier to write about these things than it is to achieve them in the very varied situations in which the Church of England is now called to function. There are places, especially in inner-city areas, where to suggest any kind of forward looking programme to the priest and the congregation is an extremely harsh form of cruelty, since they are preoccupied with simply keeping alive. A drowning man can hardly be invited to sign a contract for the building of a fine new house. There are also priests whose background, training and experience have not equipped them to give the form of leadership appropriate to the society in which they are required to work. All dioceses now offer some form of post-ordination training, but it is generally very meagre and compares badly with the continuous training offered in many other professions. In any case, the majority of the Church of England's clergy have had no further training of any kind since the day they left their theological colleges. Lack of money, time and stimulus have in many instances combined to ensure that a priest will go for years without reading a serious book.

Immediate attention should, therefore, be given to the equipping and re-equipping of the clergy. The present era is one in which the laity are beginning to play a fuller part in the life of the Church of England at every level. This is important and the process needs to be accelerated. But this does not mean that the priest has become re-dundant. On the contrary, he is more than ever necessary and his role is more challenging and exacting than at any other time during the past thousand years. He is the man whose reflective and co-ordinating skills enable the laity to function more effectively as the church in the neigh-bourhood. Translated into industrial terms, the priest combines the functions of the research scientist and the personnel manager. An inadequately trained priest is in the present circumstances worse than no priest at all, and although entry standards have been raised and courses revised in recent years, a very high proportion of those now being ordained possess neither the intellectual qualities nor the professional expertise which church leadership now demands. It would be quite disastrous for the Church of England if the continuing decline in the number of those offering themselves for ordination were to lead to a lowering of entry standards or a weakening of theological training. Which is not to assert that high academic qualifications are essential to priesthood. Bishop Mervyn Stockwood has invited the parishes of Southwark diocese to nominate certain laymen for ordination, on the understanding that they will undergo a period of training in their leisure time and continue in secular employment afterwards. There is good reason for believing that a new pattern of priesthood will result from developments of this kind, though it would be wise to recognize that there are serious limits to the amount of service that can be offered by men who already have exacting full-time jobs, and if there is to be a growth in the number of auxiliary priests the need for more able and better trained professional priests will become more, not less, pressing. Here it may be noted that the supply of men for the ministry has not altogether dried up, as appears to be the case with the Roman Catholic Church in some parts of Europe. Upwards of three hundred men are being ordained every year and if each of these (or at least as many of them as could receive what was offered) were to be given a first-class training, with the promise of equally good post-ordination training spread over their entire working lives, the Church of England would begin to experience a quality of ministerial leadership appropriate to the demands which the 20th century is now making upon all the churches. The Church of England is not a commercial undertaking, but like any large concern it neglects the training of its leaders at its peril and must always resist the temptation to substitute short-term gains for long-term progress. If financial pressures are to reduce the number of men who can be accepted for ordination – as seems certain during the coming years – the case for raising standards for those who are to be ordained is strengthened even further. And, although the effects of such a policy would eventually be profound, it could be initiated without anything approaching a revolution. Standards have been raised in the past; they can be raised again, and, although the plans for reorganizing the theological colleges are much less satisfactory than those originally proposed, the Church of England still possesses the resources to give its priests a first-class training if it believes this to be important.

More adequate training of the ordained ministry will not of course solve immediate problems, nor those to be faced during the next two decades. Neither will it, by itself, solve any problem at all. Strengthening of the priesthood must be accompanied by a strengthening of the structure within which the priest and every local church is required to operate. By the end of this century it may be anticipated that the Church of England will have considerably fewer local bases than at present. Parishes will continue to exist but most of them will be larger – geographically and in population. This need not be seen as a defeat. On the contrary, strategic withdrawal is often the prelude to advance, and there is almost everything to be said for the Church of England having fewer, but better-manned and more vigorous, parish bases. Resistance to the rationalization of its present manpower and buildings has precluded reorganization along these lines in the immediate future, but financial considerations will have a powerful effect upon the situation as the 1970s advance and there is an inevitability about the broad pattern which is to emerge. The question at issue is how this pattern will be moulded and this raises at once a further question about management or, as the church prefers to call it, pastoral care.

A very wide gap exists between those responsible for the leadership of parishes and those responsible for the leadership of dioceses. An average English diocese has about 300 parishes in an area approximating to, and sometimes coinciding with, that of a county. If the bishop has four weeks of holiday and one day off every week, he must visit one of his parishes every day in order to be seen in all of them once a year. But such a schedule is quite impossible because bishops have many other things

to attend to. Regular journeys to London for the General
Synod, the House of Lords, Bishops' Meetings and committees absorb a great deal of time. So do diocesan meetings, contacts with the secular leadership of the area and
the very considerable amount of administrative work that
inevitably lands on a bishop's desk. A bishop's diary is an
'obscene' document in its revelations of the demands made
upon a human being and in its disclosure of the un-
availability of a bishop for the primary task for which
he was consecrated. If there is a suffragan bishop, there
is just a chance that either he or the diocesan bishop may
be able to pay a brief visit – possibly to take part in an
act of worship – to every parish once a year, though very
few bishops attempt this and even fewer accomplish it.
In any case, brief visits of this kind are of very limited
usefulness. They are nothing to do with leadership and,
since the bishop has only a sketchy knowledge of the
parish, he is hardly in a position to offer much in the way
of advice or inspiration. The episcopal 'flag' is displayed
and a car is waiting impatiently to whip the bishop off
to the next port.

This arrangement is, in part, deliberate. The Church
of England does not conceive of itself as a closely-knit
organism. It is 11,000 independent corporations bound
together in a loose federation, acknowledging allegiance
to a bishop but conceding to him the minimum of
authority. Every parish priest expects, and is expected, to
get on with his work without external assistance or
interference. The bishop is there if an unmanageable crisis
arises but he is not normally to be involved in the life
of the parish, even though at every service for the instituting of a new vicar he declares himself to be responsible
for the care of the people in that place. Many of the
clergy, especially the over-50s, would not welcome frequent episcopal visitations since it would appear that
their personal freedom was being threatened. Similarly,
many bishops believe that their clergy should, in the
immortal words of Prime Minister Edward Heath, 'be able
to stand on their own two feet'. Frequent consultation
suggests that a priest is weak and in need of nursing.
Delegation of responsibility in this fashion has many

virtues and the work of the best Anglican parish priests is ample testimony to the scope which a high degree of independence affords. But it is essentially a system for a settled and stable organization where the work to be tackled is consistent and therefore predictable. When bishops could only visit the parishes of their (then much larger) dioceses on horseback or by carriage, very little was seen of them, but this was of small consequence since the life of a parish hardly changed from one century to the next.

In a rapidly changing society, when local churches are being subjected to new and particularly challenging pressures, a more integrated form of leadership becomes important. The kind of changes which will take place in the organization of the Church of England during the remaining years of this century cannot be effectively managed by small, independent units whose members are unable to see the whole picture and are in any case preoccupied with their own responsibilities. On the other hand, these changes cannot be managed from remote diocesan centres where knowledge of local situations is limited and personal contact is too infrequent to establish the degree of confidence necessary for the acceptance of change. The glaring need is for a new form of 'middle-management' to provide effective links between parochial and diocesan leadership. Attempts to meet this need have been made in recent years by bringing Rural Deans into closer relationship with the central organization of the diocese, but these have been only partially successful, partly because the majority of Rural Deans have their own heavy parochial responsibilities and partly because it is recognized on all sides that the status of the Rural Dean is not sufficient to provide him with an acknowledged leadership role, whether viewed from the angle of the parish or the diocese. The question of status is important. The only forms of leadership acknowledged within the Church of England are those of the priest (within his parish) and the bishop (within his diocese or equivalent jurisdiction). The authority of Archdeacons, Canons, Rural Deans and other functionaries has never counted for much, and bishops have never

been able to delegate more than a small amount of
responsibility to them. There may be strange and un-
Christian reasons behind this, but there is also deeply
embedded in Anglicanism a conviction that there are
only two permanent orders of ministry – priest and
bishop – and that the primary role of the bishop is one of
pastoral oversight. Such convictions cannot easily be
disregarded – nor should they be, for they are fundamentally sound.

The new 'middle-management' must, therefore, be
episcopal if it is to be effective. One bishop for every
thirty parishes would be somewhere near the ideal and,
following the reorganization of local government, it might
well be possible to arrange episcopal areas to coincide
with the boundaries of the new District Councils. The
creation of new dioceses is unnecessary and, in most cases
highly undesirable, for in many circumstances the policy
with the boundaries of the new District Councils. The
bishops would have responsibility for a defined area but
would be members of a diocesan episcopal college in
which the bishop of the whole diocese had pre-eminence.
Additional bishops would be needed to exercise oversight
of areas of special interest. In some cases the local, or
auxiliary, bishop might have responsibility for a small
parish, in others he would be detached, but in no case
would he be provided with a palace or any of the other
trappings of episcopal office in England. His leadership
role would be exercised in virtue of the authority given
to him by the church as a whole, and through his vision
and skill as a servant of the churches committed to his
care. What is here proposed is no more than an extension
of the arrangement which already exists in certain large
dioceses where suffragan bishops are given a very high
degree of responsibility within a defined episcopal district.
A change in the law would be necessary to enable the
Church of England to consecrate auxiliary bishops, thus
avoiding the need to create new diocesan or suffragan
sees, but to seek Parliamentary approval for such a proposal could hardly be considered an outrageous demand
and would provide an interesting test of the state's will-
ingness to allow the church to order its own affairs.

Once the law was altered, the introduction of the new auxiliary bishops could, in accordance with Anglican custom, begin gradually. As opportunity arose, an episcopal area would be defined – in relation to the ultimate division of the whole diocese – and a priest consecrated as a bishop. These men would be chosen from amongst the most able priests, of whom the Church of England still has a fairly ample supply, and entrusted with the leadership of the church in the area. They would be responsible for encouraging co-operation between the parishes and for renewing the church's vision of what it might become in the life of the community. When financial and other problems required a building to be declared redundant and parish boundaries adjusted, the local bishop would naturally be deeply involved in the decision-making process. His ultimate aim would be the creation of an appropriate number of strong church bases in the area, served by a variety of ministries – full-time, part-time and specialist. This would not be easy, and the history of the Church of England would guarantee strong resistance from various quarters, but the circumstances of the next few decades will make certain changes in church life unavoidable and it is therefore of crucial importance that these should be subject to control which is both local and visionary. With the increasing pressure on resources of manpower, money and buildings, co-ordination of effort and sharing of insight will become imperatives. The ecumenical implications of this are obvious.

In the light of the formidable problems which combine to present the Church of England with a deep crisis, the suggestion that the situation can best be met by better training of the clergy and the multiplication of bishops might appear to be so modest as to verge on the ludicrous or the irresponsible. Certainly it is modest – and quite deliberately so. It is of course important for the health of the church that young men should continue to have visions and that old men be permitted to dream dreams. Those responsible for ordering the life of the church must constantly be challenged with pictures of the Christian community as it ought to be. The need is for more, not less, radicals in the ranks. But it is totally unrealistic to suppose that the Church of England will accept and implement a massive programme of radical reform during the next thirty years. It will not accept such a programme; it is incapable of implementing such a programme. Those who can produce only radical and dramatic solutions to current problems will, therefore remain largely without influence, though their challenge to complacency and compromise is important. All the signs are that the death of the diseased organs in the body of the Church of England will be slow, rather than sudden. Slow death is never pleasant and is normally agonizing. It calls for deep faith, great courage and unusual sensitivity. When these qualities are displayed it can be remarkably creative for all concerned. If they are absent, all hell is let loose. The difference is between a dying life and a living death.

Given the prognosis of a lingering death to many of the church's inherited limbs and organs – though not, let it be emphasized, to the church itself – the most urgent, as well as the most practical, need is to create the conditions in which faith, courage and sensitivity can be strengthened. Nothing can, of course, take the place of the renewal and deepening of that commitment to Christ upon which the church is built and without which it cannot survive. But good leadership and appropriate organization count for a good deal at any time, and especially in a time of crisis. Such strength as the Church of England now possesses is concentrated in the life of its local churches and it is here that it must be maintained and enriched. Many of the problems which now occupy the stage at the centre of the church's life appear to be intractable and will only be solved with the passage of a long period of time. Little can be done to hasten this process, for the problems run deep. But a good deal can be done to facilitate creative development in the parishes and this requires the effective mobilization of the resources which now exist at the local level. Here it is that attention must now be concentrated and maximum use made of the facilities and freedom which stand waiting to be exploited. It will continue to be the duty of a quite small number of people to grapple in the General

Synod and elsewhere with the major signs of crisis which have occupied the greater part of this book. They will need sympathy and support. Yet the main thrust of renewal will have to move away from the centre of the Church of England's organization to the parishes, rural deaneries and dioceses where many opportunities still remain. The seizing of these opportunities will not necessarily increase the active membership of the Church of England or turn its present poverty into riches. But imagination and energy can still lead to the creation in every part of England of communities of Christians who love God and love their neighbours. This has been the vocation of the Church of England in the past. It remains the vocation of the Church of England today. And so it will continue while there is a church to serve and express the aspirations of the English people.

Index

Advisers, Archbishops', 137, 139, 149, 160.

Advisory Board for Redundant Churches, 145f.
see also Church Buildings, redundant.

Advisory Council for the Church's Ministry, 47, 106.

Africa, Christianity in North, 11.

Anglican-Methodist Unity, 9, 12, 14ff, 22f, 57, 69, 98f, 112, 130.

Anglican-Roman Catholic International Commission, 15.

Anglo-catholicism, 20ff, 58, 71, 74, 130.

Annual Parochial Meeting, 45, 125.

Appeals, Building restoration, 140ff.

Archbishops, Appointment of, 93, 99ff.

Archdeacons, 62, 185.

Articles of Religion, 18, 87.

Attendance, Church, 33, 40ff, 56, 71.

Augustine, St., of Canterbury, 94.

Baptism, 32, 42f, 124, 128, 174.
see also Services, Baptism.

Barry, F. R., 162.

Battersea, Deanery of, 144f.

Bell, G. K. A., 101f.

Benefice Income,
see Endowments, Glebe.

Birmingham,
Bishop of, 106.
Diocese of, 56.

Bishops,
Appointment of, 96f, 99f, 104ff, 108, 111, 142.
Auxiliary, 186f.
Diocesan, 26, 74, 153, 176.
House of, 14, 67f, 81, 127f.
see also House of Lords.
Role of, 31, 80f, 115, 119, 183ff.
Suffragan, 104f, 108, 184.

Board for Mission and Unity, 171.

Book of Common Prayer, 12, 18, 70, 73, 76, 78f, 81, 85, 87ff, 108, 124.
see also Prayer Book, revision of.

Booth, Charles, 27.

Boulard, F., 27.

Bridge, A. C., 89f.

Brown, Laurence, 106.

Bunsen, Bernard de, 147.

Cadogan, Alexander, 101.

Canon Law, 101, 123.

Canterbury,
Archbishop of, 68, 79, 95, 97, 99ff, 135, 145, 153, 161ff.
see also Davidson, Randall.
Fisher, Geoffrey.
Ramsey, Michael.
Temple, William.
Convocation of, 74, 76, 79, 101, 115, 119, 123f, 127, 128.

Cathedrals, Restoration of, 140ff.

Central Board of Finance, 26, 149.

Central Church Fund, 121.
Central Register of Benefice Income, 137f.
Central Stipends Authority, 67.
Chadwick Commission, 106ff, 171.
Chester, Bishop of,
  see Ellison, Gerald.
Chichester, Bishop of,
  see Bell, G. K. A.
Christian Century, The, 130.
Church Assembly, 16, 22, 59, 63, 65, 67, 74, 81, 82, 84f, 98, 106, 115ff, 125ff, 130f, 147, 152f, 154f, 164, 168, 170f, 174f.
Church Buildings,
  Maintenance of, 31, 33, 52, 136, 139f, 143ff.
  New, 73, 139, 156.
  Redundant, 63f, 145ff, 156, 187.
Church Commissioners, 62, 67, 122, 171.
  Appointment of, 153f.
  Assets Committee, 154f.
  Estates Committee, 151.
  Funds of, 33, 121, 133, 136, 141, 148, 150, 153, 155ff.
  General Purposes Committee, 155.
Church House, Westminster, 14, 120, 122.
Churchill, Winston, 101.
Church Information Office, 68.
Church and State, 24ff, 93ff, 98, 106ff, 119.
Clergy, 36, 47, 56f, 67f, 73f, 95, 115, 120, 179, 184f.
  Appointment of, 58ff, 65, 68.
  Deployment of, 55, 57f, 61ff, 68, 130, 174.
  Freehold of, 61ff, 65, 95, 115.
  House of, 14, 81, 127f, 133.
  Housing of, 57f, 96, 137, 155.
  Numbers of, 31, 46f, 137.
  Ordination of, 45ff.
  and Parliament, 96, 109.
  Payment of, 33, 65, 67, 130, 136ff, 155, 174.
  Training of, 147f, 181ff, 187.
Coggan, Donald, 9, 102, 163.
Colleges, Theological, 147f, 181, 183.

Communicants,
  see Services, Communion.
Communications, 120f, 132.
Communion, Holy,
  see Services, Communion.
Conference,
  Diocesan, 126f, 131.
  Ruridecanal, 126, 129.
Confirmation, 32, 43f, 124, 174.
  see also Services.
Cornwell, Peter, 110.
Coronation, 24, 95.
Council on Foreign Relations, 171.
Coxon, Anthony P. M., 26.
Cranmer, Thomas, 81, 87, 90f, 97.
Crockford's Clerical Directory, 60, 125.
Crown, The, 58, 95, 99f, 102f, 108, 110, 127, 131, 142, 153.

Davidson, Randall, 100f, 117.
Deaconess, 138.
Deans, 142.
  Appointment of, 96, 99f.
Dix, Gregory, 75f.
Doctrine, 18f, 80f, 84, 86f, 96f, 108, 111, 119, 123, 128.
  Archbishops' Commission on, 82f, 87, 166.
Durham, Bishop of, 24, 95, 150, 163, 165f.
  see also Harland, Maurice.
      Henson, Hensley H.
      Ramsey, Ian.
      Ramsey, Michael.

Ecclesiastical Commissioners, 151f.
Electoral Roll, 32, 44f, 115, 117, 124f, 130.
Ellison, Gerald, 66f, 167.
Endowments, 57f, 64, 67, 149f, 155f.
Establishment,
  see Church and State.
Evangelism, 20f, 22, 49, 58, 74, 82f, 85, 105, 130.
Evans, Christopher F., 169.
Evening Prayer,
  see Services, Evening.
Expenses,
  Clergy, 138f, 150.
  Parish, 139.

Faith and Order Conference, 1964, 22.
Finance, 33, 57, 121, 135ff, 183.
see also Central Board of
Fisher, Geoffrey F., 101f, 122, 163, 165, 174.
Fleming, Launcelot, 105.
Fletcher, Lord, of Islington, 146.
Freehold, Parson's, 61ff, 65, 95, 115.

Garbett, Cyril F., 25, 101, 116, 163, 167f.
Glebe, 67, 150f.
Gore, Charles, 124.
Graham, Billy, 49.
Gregory the Great, 10.
Group and Team Ministries, 63f, 156.
Guildford, Dean of
see Bridge, A. C.
Bishop of,
see Reindorp, George.

Harland, Maurice, 165f.
Headlam, A. C., 172f.
Hebert, A. G., 73, 75ff, 85.
Henson, Hensley H., 97.
Hereford, Diocese of, 55f.
Historic Churches Preservation Trust, 143.
Hodson Commission 124ff, 131f.
Holland, Henry Scott, 116.
Hooker Craigmyle & Co. 140ff.
House Groups, 28f, 91, 164, 179.
House of Commons, 12f, 24f, 80, 95, 109, 131.
House of Lords, 24, 80f, 95, 108, 164, 184.
Howick Commission, 102f, 107.
Hügel, F. von, 18f.

Incumbents (Discipline) Measures 1947-53, 62.
Investments,
see Church Commissioners, funds of.
Iremonger, F. A., 116f, 120.

James, Eric A., 172f, 175f.
Jasper, Ronald C. D., 89, 172f.

Keble Conference Group, 173f.
Kingdom of God, 50ff.

Laity, 44f, 72, 96, 114ff, 118, 121ff, 125f, 132, 136f, 179, 181.
House of, 14, 26f, 81, 115, 123f, 127f.
Lambeth Conferences, 16, 84f.
Lang, Cosmo Gordon, 97.
Leicester, Bishop of, 107.
Life and Liberty Movement, 115ff, 120, 174.
Liturgical Commission, 79ff, 85, 89, 91, 173.
Liturgical Movement, 73, 75ff, 84, 174.
Liturgy,
see Services.
London,
Bishop of, 95.
Diocese of, 41f, 55f, 130, 142, 162.

McBrien, Richard P., 50.
Mackinnon, Donald, 101f.
Manchester, Bishop of, 67.
March, Earl of, 171.
Mayfield, Guy, 125.
Methodist Church,
see Anglican-Methodist Unity.
Miskin, A. B., 54ff.
Morgan, David M. J., 26,
Morley Commission, 57, 61, 65ff, 130, 168.
Morning Prayer,
see Services, Morning.

New Christian, 175.
New Synod Group, 130.
North India, Church of, 14.
Norwich,
Bishop of, 105.
Churches of, 144, 146.

Ordinal, 87, 128.
Orthodox Churches, 92, 164.
Oxford, Diocese of, 55f.
Oxford Movement, 71.

Parish Appointment Committees, 68.
Parish and People Movement, 77, 130, 163, 171, 173f.
Parliament, 9, 24, 74, 77, 80f, 96f, 109f, 112, 115, 118, 127, 186.

Parishes,
  Community role of, 34f, 37f,
    134, 180, 188.
  Income of, 33, 57, 148ff.
  Reorganisation of, 63f, 156,
    183, 187.
  Statistics relating to, 30f, 54ff.
Parochial Church Council, 33,
  81, 115, 119, 124ff, 130, 132,
  139.
Parochial System, 54.
Partners in Ministry, 57, 67.
Pastoral Committees,
  Church Commissioners, 156f.
  Diocesan, 63f, 65, 145.
Pastoral Measure, The, 63f, 106,
  145f.
Paton, David M., 78.
Patronage, 58f.
Paul, Leslie.
  see Paul Report.
Paul Report, 26, 30, 46, 55, 61,
  65.
Peel, Robert, 150f.
Pensions Board, Church of
  England, 27, 67.
Peterborough, Bishop of, 16f.
Pitt, Valerie, 107, 109ff, 157,
  159.
Pius X, Pope, 75.
Prayer Book, Revision of, 74f,
  80f, 84, 97f, 117.
Prime Minister, 93, 96, 99ff,
  104, 108, 163, 184.
Prism, 175.

Queen Anne's Bounty, 151f.

Ramsey, Ian T., 166f, 170.
Ramsey, Michael, 10, 15f, 23, 59,
  66, 78, 81, 93, 102, 162ff, 166,
  168f, 179.
Redundant Churches Fund, 146.
Reformation, 17f, 21, 84, 87, 94,
  114, 119, 143, 177.
Reindorp, George, 168.
Representative Church Council,
  115.
Ripon, Bishop of, 16.
Roberts, Oral, 49.
Robinson, John A. T., 164, 168ff.
Roman Catholic Church, 15, 20,
  27, 71, 75f, 92, 114, 118, 182.
  Rural Dean, 185.

St. Margaret's Church, West-
  minster, 12ff.
St. Paul's Cathedral, 141f.
Salisbury Cathedral, 140f.
Schools,
  Church, 139, 156.
  Sunday, 43, 139.
Scotland, Church of, 107.
Selden, John, 87.
Services,
  Baptism, 79, 83, 87, 88.
  Burial, 82f, 88.
  Communion, 12, 71ff, 77f, 83f,
    87, 128.
  Communion, attendance at, 32,
    44, 56, 71.
  Communion, Parish, 72f, 77f,
    85, 163f, 173.
  Communion, Series 2, 12, 84ff.
  Communion, Series 3, 85, 89ff.
  Confirmation, 79, 83.
  Evening, 71f, 81.
  Experimental, 80f.
  Language of, 85, 88ff.
  Marriage, 88.
  Morning, 71f, 81.
Service of Reconciliation, 15f.
Sheffield, 40f.
Sheppard, Dick, 116f.
Smith, W. Saumerez, 103f.
Southwark,
  Diocese of, 42f, 48, 55f.
  see also Stockwood, Mervyn.
Stacey, Nicolas, 40.
Standing Committee, General
  Synod, 122.
Stewardship, 148f.
Stockwood, Mervyn, 174, 182.
Sutton, Manners, 99.
Synods,
  Deanery, 127, 129f, 132.
  Diocesan, 128f, 131f.
  General, 9, 12, 22, 47, 65,
    68, 81, 85, 89, 91ff, 103, 108,
    112, 118, 124, 127ff, 131ff,
    159, 164, 173, 184, 188f.
Synodical Government, 44f,
  124ff, 162, 174.

Teesside Industrial Mission, 142.
Temple, William, 101f, 116,
  164f.
Terms of Ministry Committee,
  67.

Theodore of Tarsus, 54.
Thompson, Kenneth, 120, 133, 135.
Times, The, 135.
Tomline, George P., 99.

Uniformity, Act of, 73, 75.

Vacancy-in-See Committee, 104ff,
Vestry Meeting, 115.
Vicar or Rector,
    Freehold of, 61ff, 65, 115.
    Income of, 137ff.
    of Redundant Church, 63.
    Role of, 36, 45, 67, 184f.
    Status, of, 25, 64.

Westminster Abbey, 13f.
Wickham, E. R., 40ff.
Wilbraham, Philip Baker, 152.
Wilson, Leonard, 106.

Winchester,
    Bishop of, 25, 95.
    Cathedral, 140f.
Wood, Maurice A. P., 105.
Woods, E. S., 116.
World Council of Churches, 164,
    171.
Worship, 70ff, 96f, 108, 111,
    119, 123, 128.
    see also Services

York,
    Archbishop of, 68, 79, 95, 102,
        135, 145, 153, 163.
    see also Coggan, Donald.
                Garbett, Cyril F.
    Churches of, 144.
    City of, 41.
    Convocation of, 74, 79, 115,
        119, 123f, 127f.
    Minster, 140ff.